MARRYING FOR LIFE

The Challenge of Creating a Lasting Friendship

by
John J. Snyder, Ph.D.

R & E Publishers

This book is sold with the understanding that the subject matter covered herein is of a general nature and does not constitute legal, accounting or other professional advice for any specific individual or situation. Anyone planning to take action in any of the areas that this book describes should, of course, seek professional advice from accountants, lawyers, tax and other advisers, as would be prudent and advisable under their given circumstances.

R&E Publishers

P.O. Box 2008, Saratoga, CA 95070
Tel: (408) 866-6303   Fax: (408) 866-0825

Book Design and Typesetting by **elletro** Productions
Book Cover and Illustrations by Kaye Quinn

ISBN 0-1-56875-039-0

Library of Congress Cataloging-in-Publication Data
Snyder, John J.
    Marrying for life : the challenge of creating a lasting friendship
    / by John J. Snyder
    p. cm.
    Includes bibliographical references and index.
    ISBN 1-56875-039-0 (soft) : $11.95
    1. Marriage. 2. Communication in marriage 3. Friendship
HQ734.S7663 1993
306.81--dc20   93-12863
                                                                CIP

Designed, typeset and totally manufactured in the
United States of America.

TO MARY

my wife and dearest friend

To Dan + Maria —

A wonderful couple.

With my best wishes.

John Snyder

CONTENTS

ACKNOWLEDGMENTS

This book grew out of a course in marriage that I taught for over twenty years at King's College. I am particularly indebted to my students for their help. Their questioning has often made me rethink my ideas and do further research. Some have shared intimate details of their relationships and have given me insights that I might otherwise never have had. Among my married students, many have excellent marriages that have been an inspiration to the students and myself.

Throughout the book, I have drawn on many of my student's experiences as well as those of friends and relatives. I have used fictional names while describing them so as not to reveal the identities of any of these persons.

I am also indebted to my colleagues, particularly those in my own Department of Philosophy and Religious Studies, for sharing their ideas on many related subjects. I am blessed to work at a College where there are many gifted individuals and an atmosphere supportive of learning and research.

My deepest thanks is reserved for my wife, Mary Snyder. Words cannot express what her love and support has meant to me over the years. My deep faith in the goodness of marriage is rooted in my marriage to her. I am particularly grateful for her careful reading and editing of the text, and for her many suggestions.

INTRODUCTION

THE NEED FOR MARITAL PREPARATION

You're in love! You've met somebody special unlike anyone you have met before. You cannot imagine ever wanting to be apart. You want to get married!

However, if you are like most people today, you may also have some reservations about taking this big step. Marriage is often viewed as giving up your independence and being tied down. It includes potential problems with in-laws, family customs, children, religion, and finances. The commitment is for life and the rest of your life could be a long time!

A further problem is that marriage breakdown and divorce have become commonplace in our society. Sociologists now estimate that between 40 to 50% of all first marriages in North America will end in divorce. Second marriages have an even higher rate of breakdown. For most people, divorce is a painful reality, involving the distress of separation, custody battles and alimony payments. It usually takes several years to recover from its ravages. Some of you may already know its painful reality from a previous personal relationship. Others may have been involved in the breakup of the marriages of family or friends. The idea of being married to someone you love seems so wonderful and yet the reality for many persons is so painful.

You are not alone in being apprehensive about getting married. The high rate of marital breakdown and divorce has made all but the most romantic persons wary about marital success. Is it realistic in this day and age to hope for a lifelong marriage that is happy and fulfilling? Can the wonderful feelings that you and your partner presently have for each other be sustained throughout a lifetime or, like everything else in this throwaway society, will the two of you soon tire of each other and look for someone else?

Good marriages: are they possible any more?

In a changing society such as ours, it is difficult to predict with any assurance what the future will bring. Based on present trends, indications are that the high rate of marital breakdown and divorce will continue well into the future. The strong opposition to divorce that was once fostered by the community, the Church, the civil law, and the media has lessened as divorce has become more prevalent. Separating couples are no longer afraid of being ostracized by their family or community. Many religious persons no longer consider divorce and remarriage to be a sin and therefore are unafraid of Church sanctions should they get divorced. In fact, most Christian Churches have liberalized their teachings and now allow divorce and remarriage. Civil laws that once made divorce extremely difficult have been changed. It has now become relatively easy to get a civil divorce. The media which encouraged lifelong marriage in the past, nowadays presents it simply as one alternative among many. Divorced couples on TV and in the movies are as commonplace as happily married couples.

Traditional supports for lifelong marriage have been severely weakened. A divorce mentality exists in our society and at the moment there are no strong indications that it is about to change. Despite some efforts within the community to stem the tide, marriage breakdown resulting in high rates of divorce will be with us for some time to come.

However, the fact that so many marriages are breaking down does not mean that good marriages do not exist. There are many good marriages. I know many couples who have them and I am sure that you do as well. I would even venture to say that the large majority of couples who do stay together have good marriages. Many studies would confirm my contention. I am also of the opinion that today's good marriages are probably better on the whole than the good marriages of the past. They are better in the sense that they are more intimate, more egalitarian and the partners work harder in preparing for them.

Let us return to the original question: Is it reasonable nowadays for a couple to hope for a good lifelong marriage? The answer is yes, but it is a qualified yes. Good marriages are possible but they do not just happen. They are not a matter of luck, fate or divine ordination. Persons who intend to marry need to be well prepared both as individuals and as a couple. Once married, they must be willing to work at making their union fruitful and lasting.

A high level of personal development is required on the part of both persons. If one or both partners are immature, they will not be able to handle the responsibilities and intimate lifestyle that come with marriage. The two partners also need to spend enough time together before marriage to come to know each other well and to determine if they want to spend a life together as a married couple. They need to discuss their individual expectations of marriage with each other and to agree on the basic outlines of their relationship. Before the marriage, and afterwards, the pair must be willing to work at their union. Both must work at it; one person alone cannot create the relationship.

At a time when traditional supports for marriage have been severely eroded and a divorce mentality pervades our North American society, the couple that is unprepared for marriage will have less chance of success. Romantic and sexual attractions will not be enough to see them through the difficult times in the union. Good marriages do and will exist but they require good preparation and a real mutual effort. It is reasonable to hope for a good marriage but that hope must be realistically grounded.

The need for premarital preparation

Is special preparation for marriage really needed? Our parents and grandparents who married in previous generations did not go through any elaborate marriage preparation. They did not take premarriage courses nor did they spend hours together reflecting on their suitability for marriage. They fell in love and after an appropriate time they got married. It was that simple. Their marriages seemed to turn out well. If that is the case, why is premarital preparation so important nowadays?

The basic fact is that our expectations of marriage have changed in recent years, as has the climate in which marriage exists. We see marriage differently and seek more out of it. Furthermore, the basic supports for lifelong marriage, as we have seen, either no longer exist or have been severely weakened.

Specifically, it is important to realize that there has been a dramatic change in the past thirty years in the way couples organize and live their marriages. What was taken for granted by couples in the forties, fifties and even the early sixties is no longer so obvious.

For example, in the past, marital roles were quite rigid. The husband was the primary breadwinner. The wife usually did not work outside the home especially when she had younger children. Nowadays, there are many options open to a couple. Although some couples still follow the traditional pattern, an increasing majority are both working outside the home, even when the children are small. In a small but growing number of cases, the husband may stay home with the children during the early years or even permanently. Flex-time or job-sharing arrangements now exist allowing both to work part time and to share the child-rearing functions.

Household chores are also shared in new ways. It is no longer assumed that the wife will do the cleaning, cooking and laundry, and that the husband will mow the lawn, fix the car and do the household repairs. These tasks may be divided in a variety of ways. Child care, once the primary responsibility of the wife, is also shared in new ways. Husbands are expected to be more fully involved in raising their children.

Having children, once taken for granted, is another expectation being seriously challenged by some couples. A growing minority of newlyweds are choosing to be childfree.

These concerns, and there are many others, can no longer be ignored by a couple when they consider marriage. In previous generations, most couples had similar marital expectations. Nowadays, with so many alternatives present, it is imperative for a couple to spend considerable time together discussing these issues, otherwise they may discover after they have married that they have diametrically opposed views in significant areas, leading to serious problems in their relationship.

Secondly, and perhaps even more significant, over the last century, more and more persons look to marriage as the primary source of intimacy in their lives. In a society that has become increasingly urban, mobile and impersonal, persons are spending less time with their families and friends than in previous generations. When an individual lives in one city and his or her family lives in another, it is hard to maintain close ties. Similarly, when long time friends are constantly on the move seeking better employment opportunities, as is so often the case nowadays, it becomes difficult to sustain these friendships. The result is a greater emphasis on marriage to provide intimacy.

The increasing number of people living in large metropolitan centers further contributes to the desire for greater closeness within marriage. Large cities tend to be highly impersonal. Although we relate to many persons on a daily basis, most of these relationships are functional and at best polite. We deal with bank tellers, store clerks, service station attendants, fellow workers, and residents in large apartment houses, but few, if any, of these associations are close. As a result, in the absence of close friends and family, for a growing number of persons, their marriages become the principal source of intimacy in their lives. They look to their partners to share their deepest thoughts and feelings. Oftentimes, there is no one else.

The growing egalitarianism between men and women is an additional factor contributing to this greater desire for intimacy between marital partners. In the past, the differing role expectations of husbands and wives meant that they often lived in different worlds. His world was the world of business, politics and sports. Hers was the world of the household, the family and the school. Closeness between the spouses was often restricted due to the sharp gap between their sexually defined worlds. Although there was some overlap, it was common for men to look to other men to share many of their basic thoughts and feelings since their wives were not familiar with certain significant aspects of their lives. The same was true for the women.

The growing egalitarianism of our society has increasingly broken down this tendency. Men and women share more common interests. More husbands participate in the running of the household and the care and education of their children. More wives are better educated, work outside the home and actively participate in business, politics and sports. As a result, contemporary couples enter marriage expecting to share more of their lives. They expect greater intimacy within their union.

This increasing tendency to see marriage as the seat of intimacy in a couple's lives is a admirable ideal. However, the expectation that marital partners will attain a high degree of intimacy is a difficult one that only a minority of couples can achieve. Having romantic feelings for each other and being sexually intimate may bring a couple together in the beginning, but romance and sexual intimacy are not the same as being personally intimate. Personal closeness is much more demanding. It takes time and effort. Both partners must be open, honest, respectful of each other, responsible, caring, and fully committed to the relationship. They need to be adaptable and to have good lines of communication. Many persons are simply not prepared to share so much of themselves. The current high rates of marital incompatibility testify to how hard it is for a couple to be so close.

Thirdly, as indicated earlier, there has been a significant erosion of traditional marital supports during the last thirty years. The strong encouragement exerted by the community, the Church, the law, and the culture for a couple to remain together and work out a difficult marriage is no longer as potent. This means that persons who encounter difficulties in their relationship will have to rely more on themselves to make their marriage work. If their initial bond is not strong, they will not have the outside support to help them work through the usual problems that arise in marriage.

These changes in contemporary marital expectations and support clearly require a couple to be better prepared for marriage than their parents and grandparents. Building a good lifelong union is more complicated nowadays.

For most couples, the period before marriage is critical for establishing the foundations of their marriage. It is the time for coming to know each other, developing solid lines of communication and discovering whether their love for each other is more than a passing romantic or sexual fancy. It is the time for discovering whether they have the same expectations, working out any major difficulties within their relationship and determining if they are truly committed to their relationship. The mutual love, awareness and commitment developed during this period will strongly shape their marriage for years to come.

Of course, this is not to say that if a couple have not prepared well, they cannot have a good marriage. Nor is it to say that if they have prepared well for their marriage, they will not have future problems. Like any other major commitment in life, the more knowledgeable a person is before making it, the more likely it is that the commitment will be realized. Ultimately, it becomes a question of improving the odds.

The purpose of this book

The intent of this book is to help you and your partner to prepare better for your forthcoming marriage. During the following pages, several important issues that should be discussed before marriage will be considered. Needless to say, not every issue of importance can be discussed but I have focused on those areas that are the most troublesome for marrying couples. My hope is that you and your partner will read these reflections, discuss them together and work out mutually agreeable solutions where difficulties arise.

This book can best be used by reading and discussing one chapter at a time. Both of you should read the chapter before you begin discussion. In discussing the material in each chapter, try to keep your thoughts from becoming too abstract. General theories are interesting but they are not always helpful in revealing how each of you really think about a particular question. For example, when talking about children, it may be interesting to discuss the pros and cons of whether children can add to a marriage or whether a marriage can be fulfilling without children. However, somewhere in your discussion, you must stop talking about these matters in generalities and begin to reveal your own feelings on the topic. Do *you* want to have children? Do *you* like children? Do *you* see children as helping or hindering your life together? It is one thing to agree in principle that a marriage can be helped by children; it is another to come to grips with whether your marriage will be more fulfilling through having children. To aid your discussion, at the end of each chapter I have included some specific questions designed to help focus your consideration.

In reflecting on these questions, bear in mind there are no absolute right or wrong answers. Each couple is unique and must work out their relationship in their own special way. What is an answer for the two of you may not be an answer for another couple. For example, you and your partner may have traditional values about the sharing of household work. You may both believe that it is best for the wife to do the cooking, the housework and the child care, and for the husband to take care of the car, the yard and the finances. Another couple may believe that it is better for the couple to divide all duties equally around the home. No study has shown conclusively that one approach is better than the other. I have seen both arrangements work well. What is important is that the two of you know what you both want and are able to work out a mutually agreeable solution. The solution must be right for you. It is your marriage.

Summary

Despite the high rate of marital breakdown and divorce in our society, a person can expect to have a good marriage. However, it is not something that will just happen. The fairy tale dream of meeting Prince Charming or Princess Aurora, falling in love and living happily ever after is just that, a fairy tale. Good marriages are created; they are not simply a matter of luck or waiting for the right person to come along. The time spent together before a couple marry is critical in establishing the foundations of their marriage. It is the period when they determine their mutual compatibility and begin the lifelong work of building a strong relationship. Preparing well for a marriage is not a luxury. It is vital to its future success. This book is designed to help a couple prepare for their marriage.

DISCUSSION QUESTIONS

1. In a time of high marital breakdown, why do I believe that our marriage will succeed when others will not?

2. Do we really need further preparation for our marriage? If not, why not?

CHAPTER ONE

LOVE: THE HEART OF A RELATIONSHIP

Most persons in our society marry because they are "in love." I know few persons nowadays who would even consider getting married if they did not have a strong love relationship. Love is at the heart of their wish to be together. It is what binds them together and makes them want to stay together. Other attractions, like sexual desire, common interests or an increase in status, may also draw a couple together. However, love is the strongest bond. If love is lacking, most persons would not marry.

Love is a most mysterious reality. It can never be fully comprehended and defined. Our efforts to grasp its full meaning will inevitably fail because love is ultimately a reality that exceeds our understanding. Just when we think we have comprehended its meaning, further experiences bring us new insights into its being. Unlike a geometrical triangle, whose nature and properties can be fully understood and defined, there is always more to learn about love.

Further ambiguities arise because we describe so many different feelings and actions as being love. We say things like: "I love my dog;" "Cars love Shell;" "Sally loves her new stereo;" "Grandma loves me;" "It's only puppy love." In each case, we use the term "love" to describe feelings that are similar but not quite the same. In some cases, the differences are slight; in others, they are quite large.

These diverse feelings we call "love" can also occur together, and often do. For example, in some relationships, romantic sentiments, sexual attraction and deeper caring feelings co-exist. It is sometimes difficult to distinguish between them. This leads to further problems of defining what love actually is.

This ambiguous character of love has led some writers on marriage to say love is so enigmatic that it is not worth discussing. As a result, they write little or nothing about it. Instead, they emphasize qualities like communication, equality and commitment. Although I agree that these latter traits are extremely important for a good marriage, I think that a caring love colors all of these qualities in a very significant way. Without love, communication, role sharing and commitment would at best be functional traits.

To illustrate, good lines of communication are important in any relationship. It is possible, however, to communicate clearly but in a destructive way. If I am mean spirited, I might tell my wife that she looks as "big as a house" in her new dress. I may be truthful, but the main intent of my remarks is to hurt her feelings. If I love my wife, I would want her to know that her new dress does not become her, but I would also go out of my way to tell her tactfully with as little hurt as possible. Good communication is important in a marriage, and it implies care and consideration.

In discussing marriage, then, it is important for us to reflect about love and its fundamental role in the union. We shall begin by distinguishing between four types of love that commonly exist among couples. Each will be described in some depth. They will also be analysed in terms of their appropriateness for providing a strong foundation for a marital relationship. In this chapter, three of these modes will be considered: romantic love, sexual love and utilitarian love. In the following chapter, self-giving love will be discussed.

Romantic love

Most persons have experienced what I am calling "romantic love" at some time during our lives.[1] Its beginnings are quite simple. Someone of the opposite sex suddenly becomes attractive in a mysterious and special way. It may be someone you have just met or it could even be a person you have known for years. A certain spark occurs and you feel strangely drawn towards him or her. In the presence of the other, you feel excited and happy. When you are apart, you often think about the other. The attraction is not primarily sexual although the other's sexual and physical attributes are usually part of what draws you to him or her.

In time, if the other person gives you any sign of reciprocation, your feelings of attraction become stronger. You begin to think about him or her continuously. Events that have occurred between you are continually replayed in your mind. You remember every word of last night's brief conversation as well as every gesture. The other now becomes the primary and exclusive object of your affection.

These initial strong feelings can become even more intense if any obstacles are placed in the way of your love. For example, as any reader of *Harlequin Romances* knows, any doubts about the other's love for you just serve to intensify your feelings. Social, religious or parental objections also tend to strengthen your feelings for the other. Ironically, criticisms about the inappropriateness of the union just heighten the feelings rather than diminish them. Parents who are trying to break up their child's relationship often achieve just the opposite.

At this stage, your yearnings for the other can become so strong that it is almost impossible to suppress them. You begin to dote on the other, thinking about them constantly. During this time, in the name of love, it is not uncommon to perform what might seem to others to be irrational acts. In *My Fair Lady*, Freddie walks up and down the street where Eliza lives every night in hopes that she may "suddenly appear." I have seen young men hitchhike a thousand miles and back over a weekend just to spend a single day with their girlfriends.

The more your love is reciprocated, the more ecstatic you become. You feel as though you are "walking on cloud nine." However, if your love is not returned, intense pain and emptiness is experienced. These strong feelings of joy or emptiness can last for months, even years. They will subside only when your romantic feelings are replaced by a more caring love or it becomes clear there is no real hope of reciprocation. The spurned lover may carry a "torch" for some time but if all hope is gone, the flame will eventually flicker out.

The ultimate goal of a romantic love relationship is to have your partner love you in the same way that you love him or her. You want the other to make an exclusive commitment to you and to maintain forever the heightened fervour of the relationship. Having a sexual relationship is not the main objective, although for many couples, sexual intercourse is the ultimate sign of their mutual emotional commitment.

Most of you, I am sure, have experienced the ups and downs of romantic love. I know I certainly have. It is a common form of love that is experienced by most persons within our society. Although it is especially prevalent among the young, it is also found among older persons. I have met senior citizens who have had intense romantic feelings for each other, often to the amazement and sometimes the disgust of their juniors.

In our culture, romantic love plays a major role in mate selection. Few persons would consider marrying someone if they did not have romantic feelings for him or her. Without this special spark and excitement, most of us would find our relationship dull and lifeless. These strong feelings of affection draw us together and make us want to do good things for each other. They also give us a special zest for living.

Despite all its positive traits, romantic love, by itself, does not provide a sound basis for an enduring and fruitful marriage. The initial problem is that what draws the couple together are unwilled feelings that just happen. The popular phrase, "falling in love," is quite apt. You do not choose to have these feelings nor can you ignore them. You unwittingly "fall for" the other.

In the early stages of the relationship, these feelings will go away soon if you decide not to pursue them. However, once the relationship develops, they can become so intense that it is almost impossible to resist them. If you have ever "fallen in love," you know how difficult it is to put aside these feelings once they have a strong hold upon you.

When persons are mainly drawn together by these powerful unwilled feelings, they may "fall in love" with someone who is completely unsuitable as a partner. Under the influence of these irrational feelings, they may even get married. Only later, when the original ardor has cooled and the pronounced differences between them become obvious, do the couple realize that their relationship was a mistake.

I have known many couples who have met, fallen in love and quickly married only to discover in time that they did not really know each other. Under the spell of their romantic feelings, they believed the fairy tale that simply falling in love would be enough to guarantee that they would "live happily ever after." Unfortunately, the fairy tale was not true. Romantic feelings draw a couple together, but much more is needed to build a successful relationship.

Romantic love also tends to cause persons to view their partner in a highly idealized way. They do not always look at the other realistically but tend to see him or her only in the most favorable light. Positive traits are overemphasized and exaggerated. Negative traits are de-emphasized or ignored. As a result, the partners do not love the other as he or she is but only as a highly romanticized ideal.

The old saying, "love is blind," is especially true of romantic love. You blind yourself to your partner's bad traits and habits. It is not that you do not see these bad traits. You do, but you put them at the back of your mind or even forget about them. I have known young women under the sway of romantic feelings who have gone out with men who were incapable of holding a job or who drank excessively. They were aware of these problems but they downplayed them, somehow believing that the wonderful feelings of love existing between them would overcome, and in time cure, these deficiencies. Needless to say, they did not. Similarly, I have known infatuated young men who have related with women who spent money like water and overtly sought the attention of other men. They knew of these problems but their romanticized view of their partners did not allow them to make an honest assessment.

If you do not perceive your partner realistically, you cannot develop an authentic relationship with him or her. When actual knowledge is lacking, imagination fills the gap. Relating to an imagined personality does not make for a genuine relationship. This unreal "persona" that you have romantically created will sooner or later cause problems for your relationship.

Romantic love, by itself, is simply too irrational and too blind to provide an adequate basis for an enduring and fruitful relationship. It needs to be accompanied by a deeper and more intimate form of love.

Sexual love

In today's society, having sexual relations with someone is commonly called "making love." When persons "make love," they may be expressing their romantic feelings or even a deeper form of love, but sometimes their primary purpose is simply sexual gratification. "Sexual love," as I will be using the term, refers to the latter. In its purest form, sexual love is a strong physical attraction for someone that aims at gratification and consummation.

Most of you, I am sure, know of relationships that are primarily sexual. You may even be hesitant to call them love relationships because they are so physically based. However, when I talk to persons in these relationships, most have no qualms about saying that they are in love. The pleasurable feelings that result from kissing, caressing and intercourse draw the couple together and give them a feeling of oneness. Their sexual closeness moves them to exchange tender words and to perform good acts for each other. They perceive their sexual bond as a love bond.

In a sexual love relationship, the original attraction that draws a couple together is blatantly physical. A common example is a couple who meet in a singles bar or a party. Their initial appeal is purely sexual. After a few drinks, they go to one or other's apartment and "hop in bed." In most cases these relationships are simply one night stands but sometimes they may develop into ongoing sexual encounters.

A relationship that is predominantly sexual need not always begin that way. Sometimes, romantic feelings or shared common interests rather than physical desires initially attract the couple. However, over time, as the couple increasingly express their feelings physically, the relationship may become dominated by long periods of sexual love-making. The physical aspects of the relationship take over and become the primary bond of the couple.

It should be noted that a sexual love relationship does not have to include sexual intercourse. Some couples because of religious or personal reasons do not believe in having sexual relations before marriage. This does not prevent them from having a relationship dominated by sexual passion. They may not have intercourse but they may engage in everything else from long periods of petting to mutual masturbation. Oftentimes whole evenings are spent rapt in fond embrace with only occasional breathers so they can "come up for air." Their kissing, necking, and petting binds them together and over time, perhaps without their realization, become their primary reason for being together.

It often happens that one partner is primarily motivated by sexual love and the other by romantic love. Usually, but not always, it is the man who seeks the sexual relationship and the woman who wants a romantic one. This occurs in our culture because men are encouraged by a strong male subculture to be sexually aggressive and to "score" sexually. Women, in contrast, are highly influenced by a female subculture that emphasizes romance. When the products of these two subcultures come together, the result is a typical relationship where he is looking primarily for sex and she is looking basically for romance.

Like romantic love, sexual love is a strong force impelling a couple to marry. It can be especially strong for couples who are waiting until marriage before they have sexual intercourse. Marriage alone will provide them with the sexual release they so urgently desire.

Sexual love, by itself, does not provide an adequate basis for an enduring and satisfying marital relationship. The union effected is primarily one of bodies, not of souls. The couple's relationship is dominated by their sexual passion. When they are together, they spend hours in sexual embrace. When they are apart, they cannot wait to be back in each other's arms. The pleasurable feelings, tender caresses and whispered "sweet nothings" give the impression of a deeper love. However, the couple really do not share much besides their compulsive desire to be together sexually. This preoccupation prevents them from coming to know each other in any other aspect or way. They do not spend the time needed to explore the non-sexual aspects of their relationship. As a result, they are ill prepared for marriage. Unless they can relate to each other as whole persons and not simply as sexual beings, their relationship will be shallow at best.

Utilitarian love

Love, for some persons, is an attraction to someone mainly because he or she fulfills their needs or deficiencies. The other is loved because he or she is in some way useful. To illustrate, a young man may see a woman as a desirable partner because she is well placed socially and her good looks impress his friends. She, in turn, loves him because he drives her around in a high performance sports car and lavishes presents on her. He has a prestigious job and enjoys a good image in the community. The primary attraction in both cases is the usefulness of the other in achieving personal status, wealth and luxury. Both need to be seen in the right places with the right people. The other is not valued in his or her own right but takes on value relative to the lover's own desires or needs.

It is strange to talk about "love" in utilitarian terms. Using someone is not a customary way of speaking about love. "She's just using him" is a common criticism of a questionable relationship. Yet, individuals commonly love each other in this way. "I love you" means "I will care for you and will treat you well, provided you serve my needs." Affection and warmth are present but only conditionally. When these needs are no longer fulfilled, love is at an end.

In the film, *An Officer and a Gentleman*, there is a good example of a warm but utilitarian love. Two young women who work in a factory near an Officer's Training School become involved with two of the men from the School. One of these women, Lynette, sees her relationship as an opportunity to improve her social status. She tells Sid that she loves him. Her relationship with him is warm and affectionate. She enjoys being with him and is thrilled when he gives her an engagement ring. However, when she discovers that he has dropped out of school and will not become a pilot, she returns his ring because she cannot bear the thought of being an ordinary housewife in a small town in Oklahoma rather than being the wife of a glamorous pilot who travels around the world. She found Sid attractive and responded warmly to him until he no longer fulfilled her dream for social status. She would describe her affection and attraction as love but this love was clearly conditioned on his becoming an officer. Her rejection of him ultimately had tragic consequences.

Utilitarian love is more prevalent than commonly believed. In a society obsessed with the attainment of material goods, it is not surprising that many persons seek partners solely to satisfy personal needs or deficiencies. Often they are well aware of their utilitarian motives, but sometimes they are unconscious of their real motive for being in the relationship.

Besides the obvious cases of being attracted to someone because he or she satisfies one's need for social status or wealth, there are several other common relationships that are essentially utilitarian in nature. A young woman might come from an unhappy home where her parents fight continually. She and her siblings may have been abused. Her life is dismal. She meets a young man who wants to marry her. She likes him but is not strongly drawn to him. Her main attraction to him is the hope that some day he will be the instrument of getting her out of these dreadful circumstances. Consciously or unconsciously, her relationship with this young man is utilitarian. She loves him because he will take her away from it all.

Another case is that of a young man who has been dating a woman for some time. He likes her but is not greatly attracted to her. His family think that she is wonderful. She is pretty, well educated, loves children, is a good homemaker, and has a charming personality. They press him to marry her. He does so, but mainly because he does not wish to disappoint his family. He has misgivings about the union but family pressures are too strong. His love for her is functional. He is fond of her but his basic attraction to her is that she pleases his parents.

A third instance is that of an unmarried woman in her early thirties who wants to marry but has not yet found a suitable partner. By chance, she meets a man who is quite taken by her. He wants to marry her. She is not that strongly attracted to him but fears he may be her last chance. Faced with the choice of years being alone or being married to someone she does not love strongly, she chooses to marry. She genuinely likes him and may even be willing to say that she loves him. However, her basic attraction to him is that he serves to rescue her from what she believes will be a lifetime of loneliness.

A final example is the case of a man with a drinking problem. He meets a woman who is able to keep him "off the bottle." He likes this woman but his main attraction to her is that she helps him to remain sober. She, in turn, has her own problems. She has a poor self-image and a low level of self-esteem. When he is sober, he boosts her image and makes her feel good and useful. She likes him but mainly because he gives her confidence in herself. The couple eventually marry. The relationship is functional on both sides. He loves her mainly because she helps him to stay sober. She loves him basically because he bolsters her self-esteem.

In all of these cases, the intent of their love is to have some personal need fulfilled. Their concern for the other is conditioned on this need being fulfilled. They do not love the other as he or she is, but are concerned mainly about what the beloved can do for them.

Utilitarian love, by itself, cannot provide a solid basis for a fruitful and enduring marriage. Although the couple may have a more realistic perception of each other than in a romantic love relationship, and try to meet needs other than the simply sexual, the fact remains that one or both parties in the relationship are interested in the other only insofar as he or she satisfies some personal need or deficiency. This is only a partial love. There is no appreciation of the other as a whole person. The husband who loves his wife mainly because she is a good housekeeper and cook does not fully appreciate the other aspects of her personality. He will not encounter her as she really is and thus will not be able to respond to her real needs. His relationship to her can only be shallow. Furthermore, if she ceases to satisfy him or if his needs change such that she cannot satisfy them, the relationship will be in jeopardy. Utilitarian love, by itself, provides an incomplete basis for a marriage. It unites the couple in a partial union rather than in a full personal union.

The need for a deeper form of love

Clearly, romantic, sexual and utilitarian loves, taken by themselves, are incapable of providing a sound basis for a fruitful and enduring marriage. When a couple are under the spell of romantic love, they are drawn together by romanticized perceptions which are unrealistic, preventing them from coming to know each other in a genuine way. They love a facade, an image, not a real person. As a result, they are incapable of building an authentic relationship. A more realistic understanding of each other and what they both want from marriage is needed.

Sexual love, on its own, is also an incomplete love. Persons under its influence are physically drawn together but their preoccupation with sex prevents them from exploring each other's larger personalities. A physical union is effected but not a spiritual union.

Utilitarian love is inadequate as well. When a couple center their relationship on utilitarian concerns like status and material success, their love is conditioned on the fulfillment of these needs. The other is not loved as a whole but only insofar as he or she satisfies the needs of the other. If the lover is not satisfied, he or she will cease to care for the other. The relationship's conditional nature makes it shallow.

Even in combination, these modes of love cannot make for a fruitful marriage. The idealism and volatility of romantic love plus the incompleteness of sexual and utilitarian love do not add up to a full and realistic relationship. The unions may last but rarely will they be deeply fulfilling. More is needed.

These criticisms of romantic and sexual love should not be read as indicating that I think a marriage does not need romance or sex. Far from it. A romantic spark and a healthy sexual attraction are strong and positive forces in drawing a couple together. They give the relationship excitement and zest. It is a definite plus for a couple to have these exciting feelings for each other. My point is that romance and sexual desire by themselves are not enough. They are incomplete and partial expressions of love. A couple need a deeper love that responds to the full range of each other's needs.

Similarly, my criticisms of utilitarian love should not be interpreted as meaning that a couple should not try to satisfy mutual needs within a marriage. They should. However, a marriage whose existence is founded solely on satisfying immediate personal needs is on shaky grounds from the start. What is needed is a deeper and unconditional love that responds to the other person as he or she is. This love which centers on the whole person and is self-giving will be the focus of the next chapter.

DISCUSSION QUESTIONS

1. Is our relationship overly romantic?
2. Is there too little romance in our relationship?
3. Does sex play too large a role in our relationship?
4. Are there conditions attached to my love for you? Why do I really love you?

CHAPTER TWO

SELF-GIVING LOVE

Have you ever asked yourself: why do I want someone to love me? What is it about me that is lovable? Think about it for a minute.

I think most of us would like others to find us physically attractive, at least to some extent. Why else do we spend so much time on the way we appear? But, would you want others to love you simply because you are a marvellous physical specimen? It is flattering to have others appreciate your looks, but if that is all that attracts them, it surely will not be sufficient. You will want to be loved for something more than your body, no matter how great you look.

If someone had a "crush" on you and had an unreal and inflated vision of you, how long would you be content? You might be gratified that they are attracted to you, but how long would you be satisfied knowing that they love some romanticized person that you are not? How long would you be content knowing that the other did not love your real self but some phony image?

Would you want others to love you mainly because you drive them around in an expensive sports car or because you have a good job? You may hope that others will be impressed by your money or status, but ultimately I think that you will want them to love you for more than your affluence or position.

In my first year at University, I was placed in a dormitory room with the son of a famous movie star. He received much attention from those around him. It was prestigious to date or "hang out" with "the movie star's" son. It was clear that this kind of attention bothered him. He once said to me: "I want people to like me for who I am, not because I am the son of my father." I think all of us ultimately share this same feeling.

After a bit of thought, it becomes clear that none of us want others to love us simply because of our looks, money, status, family connections, ability in bed, or any other single trait. What we really want is to be loved as a whole person. We want others to appreciate us in our entirety, good, bad, successful or not. The kind of love that answers to this desire to be loved for ourselves is what I call self-giving love.[1] It is a love that responds to a person as he or she is, and seeks the person's growth and well-being.

Self-giving love may be described as an active concern for the well-being of the other. It is a willful seeking of the other's growth and development. Called "mature love" by Erich Fromm,[2] "*agape*" by C.S. Lewis[3] and Rollo May,[4] "B-Love" by Abraham Maslow,[5] and "unconditional love" by John Powell,[6] its primary focus is on the needs of the other, not the needs of the self. It is more concerned with giving than with receiving and takes more pleasure in giving than in receiving.

In a self-giving love relationship, the partners love each other for who they are in themselves. They do not love just the congenial aspects or the desirable traits of the other. They care about one another as full and entire persons. The good and the bad, the beautiful and the ugly, are seen as parts of one totality, and the whole person is loved.

Developing a love relationship

To illustrate how a self-giving love relationship develops, let us use the example of Jim and Judy, a pair of college students. Jim is initially attracted to Judy because of her looks. Although he knows little about her, he is keen to date such a striking beauty. Getting a date with her also really impresses the guys in his dorm. Judy is attracted to Jim because of his looks as well. Since Jim is prominent in campus affairs, she too is the envy of her friends. Although their initial attraction to each other is physical and somewhat utilitarian, they are open to a deeper relationship.

In time, as they come to know each other more, strong romantic and sexual feelings develop between them. They also begin to develop a more genuine appreciation of the real worth of the other. Jim sees many admirable qualities in her. He is particularly impressed by her warmth, intelligence and generosity. Judy, in turn, comes to see him as more than just a "campus mover and shaker." She is especially attracted by his wit and integrity. Although they both see some undesirable traits in the other and have occasional spats, their union continues to grow.

As the relationship develops, there is a growing appreciation and respect of each other as unique persons with their own unique ways of life. They value this in each other and are continuously moved to foster it through their actions and support. She encourages his political ambitions and supports his interests in sports. He fosters her academic studies and her interest in theatre. At the same time, Judy and Jim increasingly want to share more of their lives together. They spend more time with one another and begin to plan their future together. There is growing empathy between them as they share their mutual hopes and failures, their joys and pains. Their lives become progressively intertwined.

The love that Judy and Jim have for each other is more than a romantic or sexual love. What eventually draws them together and seals their relationship is their mutual appreciation and concern for one another as persons. Their romantic and sexual feelings do not disappear but are founded on a deeper and more lasting self-giving love.

The attraction in a self-giving love

When you love someone with self-giving love, what attracts you is the very person or self of the other. The beloved is invariably a mix of the good and the bad. You enjoy your boyfriend's sense of humor, intelligence, outgoingness, honesty, and ambition. You appreciate how he goes out of his way to be helpful to you and your family. You like the little surprise gifts he buys you, the pleasant aroma of his aftershave and the warmth of his arms around you. You admire the many good things he does. However, you are not happy with his tendency to be late, his occasional profanity, his preoccupation with fishing, and his sloppiness around the apartment. Still, all points considered, you find him very attractive and are happy to be with him.

Attractiveness is not a static trait. When persons change, they become more or less attractive. For example, over time, a young woman may come to appreciate traits in her boyfriend that were not manifest earlier. During the development of a successful small business, she admires his new found self-confidence and hard work, qualities that she did not see in him before. On the other hand, she may discover that when he drinks too much, he becomes bellicose and this unattractive trait scares her.

The union effected in a self-giving love

When you love someone with a self-giving love, you seek to identify with that person. You want to become one with him or her. You want to share in the other's personal life. You seek to know the other's innermost thoughts and feelings. You want to respond to his or her needs. The cares of the other become your cares. The more involved you are, the greater your identification with the life of the other.

A good illustration of how a person in love identifies with another can be found in the case of a mother who has a young daughter about to perform in her first ballet recital. To the mother, the young girl is not just another child about to perform her first dance. This is her daughter, and her deep affection for her little girl moves her to empathize fully with her throughout the evening. Before the dance, the mother is well aware of her daughter's anxiety. She is nervous because her daughter is nervous. When the young girl misses a step, the mother feels her daughter's embarrassment and is pained by it. After the daughter successfully dances the rest of the performance, the mother shares in the child's jubilation. She is so involved with her daughter that the joys and pains of her little girl are quite literally her own.

Similarly, as a husband grows closer to his wife, her concerns progressively become his. He identifies with her frustration when her car has mechanical problems. He suffers with her when she gets a toothache. He is jubilant when she gets a promotion. When he goes away on a business trip, his thoughts turn regularly to her. He wonders what she is doing, and how her day is going. When he goes alone to a good restaurant, he wishes that she was with him so that she could enjoy the meal as well. Her life and its concerns are a real part of his life. What he does for her, in a real sense he does for himself. Through loving her, his life becomes one with hers.

Self-giving love involves reflection and choice

When you care about someone, you want what is best for that person. However, what is best for the other is not always immediately clear. To illustrate, a husband may be aware that his wife is being unfairly treated at her office. Other persons with lesser credentials have been promoted ahead of her. He knows that she has worked hard and deserves a promotion. Does he urge his wife to stand up to her boss and demand to be promoted? Does he encourage her to look for a new job because she will never be one of the boss's "favorites?" Or does he simply commiserate with her because there is nothing that can really be done in the circumstance? He wants to support his wife, but how can he best do it? The loving course of action is not clear. Further discussion and reflection are needed.

Self-giving love is not an irrational or impulsive love. Persons are not overwhelmed by irresistible feelings that compel them to act in a certain way. At times, they need to reflect about what is the loving course of action.

Self-giving love as a disposition

To be a loving person, it is important not only to perform individual acts of love but to develop a strong orientation of character to be loving. Anyone on occasion can perform an act of self-giving love. Even the most selfish of persons may be moved at times to act on behalf of another's welfare. However, to be able to act lovingly as a usual way of being implies the development of an inner disposition to be loving. By a "disposition," I mean an acquired inner attitude or orientation of character which inclines a person to act easily and consistently in a particular way when the occasion warrants.

Do you recall, when you first began to drive, how awkward you were? Staying on the road, maintaining the right speed, checking your rear view mirrors, reading road signs, signalling, and trying to follow your instructor's panic stricken advice seemed like an overwhelming task. However, in time, you learned to coordinate all of these actions until now you do them almost automatically. Driving has become second nature to you. You no longer have to think about how to drive each time you get into a car. You already know and when the occasion arises, you are already predisposed to drive again.

Learning to drive is just one of the many ways in which we dispose ourselves to act in the future. If we did not acquire these dispositions, we would constantly have to start from scratch. Even basics, like walking, reading, counting, and speaking English would have to be continually relearned, and our lives would be incredibly tedious and unproductive.

Just as we can acquire a disposition to drive or read, so too it is possible to acquire a disposition to be loving in a self-giving way. This disposition, like other acquired dispositions, is achieved through repeated acts of love. Each time we act in a loving way, we reinforce and strengthen our initial tendency to be caring. Once a loving disposition has been developed, we will be inclined to act lovingly as a normal way of being. We will be hesitant to love only if the situation warrants a withdrawal of love.

has developed a loving attitude, he or she will never have to think about what it means to be loving in a particular situation. The disposition to love will be present but the knowledge of what is a loving act in a particular case may not be immediately present. As we have seen earlier, further reflection will be needed.

The possession of a loving disposition also does not mean that a person will automatically be loving. Having a loving attitude is not a guarantee that a person will not act in an unloving way. An acquired disposition to love does not compel a person to love; it simply makes it easier. The person is inclined to be loving, but still has to choose to love. He or she can always opt to act in an unloving way. To return to the earlier example of driving a car, just because a young man knows how to drive a car safely does not mean that he might sometimes become careless and miss a stop sign or drive too fast. It may be out of character, but sometimes we act out of character.

Continued unloving acts, whether due to selfishness or apathy, will soon destroy our original disposition to be self-giving. Returning to our example, if the young man continues to drive at unsafe speeds and perform other perilous acts, he will soon lose his basic safe driving mentality, not to mention his license. In like manner, repeated unloving acts will quickly destroy a loving attitude.

Developing a disposition to love

The disposition to love in a self-giving and caring way is normally formed in an atmosphere of love. Most persons learn to love in loving home situations. Although it may be ideal to have two caring parents, a warm single parent or one or more loving surrogate caregivers can be just as effective. The important point is that the person feels loved and is encouraged to be loving.

When you feel loved, you are not constantly seeking to be loved by someone else. You feel confident that others value you and therefore are free to devote yourself to their needs. When you do not feel loved, you feel as though you have little worth, and will be constantly looking to others to shore up your self-image. Your need to be loved will be a paramount concern and fulfilling this need will dominate your daily activity. In your relations with others, you will be more interested in receiving than in giving. Your love will be self-serving rather than self-giving. If your self-perception is poor enough, you may simply withdraw and not even want to relate with others.

As any school teacher will tell you, children who come from homes where they are unloved and unwanted, invariably have problems. Some of these children engage in disruptive activities like fights, emotional outbreaks or failure to do their homework in a desperate attempt to gain attention and affection. Others feel so insecure and unworthy that they withdraw from ordinary school activities and shun their playmates. The need for these children to be loved and respected is a primary concern and until it is satisfied, their problems will remain and intensify.

A child raised in an unloving atmosphere is undoubtedly at a disadvantage. Learning to love at a later time is much more difficult. The self-deprecating and self-centered attitudes formed during early periods have to be unlearned and replaced by new attitudes of self-respect and other-centeredness. In most cases, a deeply caring person or persons are needed to help. This could be a good friend, priest or minister, neighbor, teacher, or relative. The combined efforts of all may be required. In severe cases, therapy may be necessary.

When children are raised in an atmosphere of love, they are encouraged to be loving towards others. Loving parents teach them to be affectionate, sharing and giving. "Be nice to your sister!" "Share your toys with your brother." "Don't be selfish!" In this way, the children begin to develop a disposition to be loving. Over time, their parents, teachers and friends continue to encourage them to see others as good and to respond positively towards them. As they get older, the give and take of their closer relationships become the primary instruments of their learning to be less self-centered and more open and responsive to their peers.

It is a mistake to think that persons can enter into a new relationship with someone and can start learning from scratch how to love in a self-giving way. No relationship begins in a vacuum. If individuals have been raised in a loving atmosphere and are basically disposed to be loving persons, they will bring that predisposition into the relationship. It will positively condition their ability to act in a loving way. However, if they have been raised to be self-centered and to use other people for their own benefit, they will be primarily interested in their own welfare. When they enter into a new relationship, they will not suddenly become other-centered and self-giving. Once the initial romantic and sexual feelings wear away, their prior disposition will especially come into play. They will be more concerned about their own well-being than that of their partner. This predominantly selfish attitude will eventually cause problems in the relationship.

In time, through much give and take, a selfish attitude can be changed. However, it is difficult to change habits overnight that have been built up over a lifetime. The relationship may not be able to endure the stress and may eventually dissolve. Persons who are strongly inclined to be self-centered may have to experience many poor relationships before their attitudes can be changed sufficiently to allow for deeper and more satisfying ones.

Our need to love

All of us have a deep need not only to be loved but also to love. We need to love not just because it is a means to get others to love us. This is a functional approach. We need to love because it is our chief way of entering into the world of others. Love enables us to overcome our estrangement from others and to share in their lives. We move beyond our private world of personal thoughts and aspirations, and identify with the preoccupations and pursuits of others. Their joys, pains, hopes, and fears become our joys, pains, hopes, and fears. By making their concerns our own, we actively participate in their lives. Our lives become expanded and enriched.

Returning to our earlier example, when Jim first falls in love with Judy, he is mainly attracted by her looks and sexiness. In time, he becomes fascinated by her larger personality. He wants to know everything he can about her. He wishes to make her concerns, his own. More and more he gives of his time and energy to act on her behalf. Her happiness becomes as important to him as his own. Her world is very much part of his world. He is enriched by his love of her.

Self-giving love alone brings about a real union with others. Romantic love effects a union with an idealized and unreal person. Sexual love brings about a union of bodies, not of souls. Utilitarian love loves only a part of a person. To achieve a real union with others, we need to love and be loved in a self-giving way. Being loved and loving are not luxuries. They are essential to full human growth.

Two side effects of self-giving love

Two significant side effects of loving in a self-giving way need to be mentioned. The first is that it feels good. When you help the little old lady next door across a street, you have a good feeling inside. It is satisfying to know that you made her life easier and it is gratifying to receive her thanks. Similarly, it feels good to help your partner by going out of your way to do something special for him or her. Loving someone gives you a satisfying feeling.

The primary reason for performing an act of love, however, is not simply to receive these good feelings. The intent of a loving act is the well-being of the other. Good feelings are consequent upon achieving that goal. If achieving good feelings were the primary end of our loving acts, then it would make sense to wait by street corners so that we could receive the gratification of helping a stream of little old ladies across the street, whether they wanted to be helped or not. Their safety would not be as important to us as our own pleasure. The actions would be functional, not self-giving.

A second significant effect of self-giving love is that it is a potent force in moving others to love you. As was said earlier, loving is not done simply to receive love. However, genuine love regularly causes others to respond in kind. When love is expressed to someone, the warm approach, affectionate words and caring gestures often move others to return your love. When persons are loved by you, they feel worthwhile and valuable. They know that you are identifying with their concerns. Your willingness to act on their behalf makes you more attractive to them and is an impetus for them to respond in kind. The more you love, the greater the possibility that you will be loved in return.

Of course, the other does not have to respond to your love. He or she may be attracted to you but this does not necessitate a loving response. Love is always freely given. A response cannot be forced. More often than not, however, the result of giving love is to receive love.

Self-giving love and marriage

A marriage can last without a strong mutual self-giving love. A self-giving love may not be necessary to keep a couple together. If the pair meet basic functional needs and treat each other reasonably, they may find enough in the union to stay together. However, it is self-giving love that perfects a union. Love makes a couple want to be together. It transforms a working partnership into a true union.

Self-giving love is the heart of a good marriage. It is the underlying attitude that moves the partners to act for the well-being of each other and to share each other's lives. It is the relational power that truly enables the two to become one.

DISCUSSION QUESTIONS

1. Is your love for your partner self-giving?
2. What attracts you about your partner?
3. Is the happiness of your partner important to you?
4. If your partner should go away, what would you miss about him or her?
5. Do you try to be a loving person in your daily life?

6. Does your partner try to be a loving person in his or her daily life?

7. Was the atmosphere of your early childhood a loving one?

CHAPTER THREE

MUTUAL SELF-GIVING LOVE AND INTIMACY

When two persons love each other, their natural tendency is to want to be together. As their relationship develops, they want to become as close as possible. They desire to be intimate.

For many persons, nowadays, intimacy simply means sexual intimacy. Physical intimacy, however, is only one aspect of intimacy. Sexual closeness does not necessarily include emotional and intellectual intimacy. Having sex may be a pleasurable and exciting experience, but it does not by itself help one to know and respond to the other's deepest thoughts and feelings.

The nature of true intimacy

True intimacy involves not only a closeness of bodies, but especially a closeness of hearts and minds. It exists when two persons know and relate with each other at the depths of their being. They become familiar with each other's deepest thoughts, feelings and desires, and respond caringly to one another.

"Depth" is the key word here. It refers to those innermost ideals, desires, feelings, and motivations that are at the heart of a person and ultimately determine the main bearings of his or her personality. This private persona is usually hidden behind the numerous facades, protective barriers and roles that a person presents to the outside world. Only when these superficial levels of personality are penetrated can a relationship with the real person take place. This is a very special experience that most of us realize fully with only a small number of people in our lives.

Our need for intimacy

All of us need close friends. We need persons with whom we can relate as we are. There are not many people with whom we feel comfortable and relaxed enough to reveal private thoughts and feelings. Having a close friend who knows us and loves us in spite of our frailties, gives us the confidence to "let down our hair" and admit to our true feelings. We feel secure in revealing our selves, and are not afraid to express our deepest feelings and thoughts.

Close friends who are aware of our real nature will not be taken in by the public image we present to others. They can be bluntly honest with us when we try to play games, even to the point of "telling us off" when needed. Even though they are aware of our faults and failures, we still feel confident that they care for us and will be present for us whenever we need their help.

Having a good close friend enables us to transcend our own limited world and participate in the world of another. It helps us to overcome our separateness and to enter the richness of another's life. When we know and care for someone intimately, we truly share in his or her life and thereby expand our own world. Our life becomes more than concern about our own personal desires and thoughts. The world of the other person literally becomes part of our world. The joys and sorrows of our friend become our own joys and sorrows.

In our highly urbanized and mobile world, as mentioned before, most of our relationships are impersonal and functional. Our dealings with persons like bank tellers, store clerks, gasoline attendants, and bureaucratic government officials are usually polite but are hardly intended to be close. Even our relationships with neighbors are often conducted at a surface level due to the large size of apartments and impersonal neighborhoods. If all of our relationships were conducted at these shallow and impersonal levels, we would not be appreciated for who we really are nor would we truly share in the lives of others. At best, we would be polite strangers.

Basic characteristics of intimacy

An intimate relationship has several basic and interrelated characteristics that are *rooted in the self-giving love at its core.* As a love union, an intimate relationship implies mutual attraction, care, awareness, respect, commitment, and trust. It also presupposes a mutual willingness to make sacrifices, to forgive each other and to give one another the freedom to be oneself within a relationship. These characteristics are not simply desirable additions that make an intimate relationship better. They are central to its very being. In the absence of any of them, a continuing close union will be difficult to achieve.

Much can be written about each of these traits. At this time, our discussion will be limited to a brief description of their basic nature. Many will be discussed further in succeeding chapters.

Mutual attraction

There is a popular view that a couple have a strong attraction for each other only at the beginning of their relationship when the flames of romance and passion draw them together. It is believed that over time, these feelings will subside and the mutual attraction of the couple will diminish. This simply is not true. Couples who have a close relationship have an attraction that gets stronger over time. They are continuously drawn to the inner personality of each other. They may not manifest this attraction by constantly mooning over each other or by public displays of affection, but it is clearly present in the way they act towards each other. The partners enjoy one another and cherish their time together. They like to go out together, travel together, eat together, make love, or just sit with each other at the end of the day reading newspapers or watching television. They find each other endlessly fascinating.

Mutual care

Attracted by the inner personality of the other, the partners want one another to grow and develop in their own unique way. They respond caringly and unselfishly to the needs of the other. In times of crisis, they offer support; in times of pain, they offer consolation; and in times of loneliness, they bring warmth and tenderness.

Recently, a good friend died after a seven year battle with cancer. During the final months when she was very sick and knew that her death was coming, she and her husband spent many hours talking and reflecting together. Their love and devotion to each other was obvious. I was especially impressed by her concern for what would happen to him after she was gone. She knew him well and was aware that he would flounder without a close companion. She talked to him at some length about his need to find a new partner and urged him not to feel guilty about remarrying. She cared for him deeply, even beyond her days on this earth.

In an intimate relationship, both partners care about each other and the growth of their relationship. They are actively concerned to help one another become more fulfilled as persons. They continually do little things to make the other happy. Without her asking, he washes and cleans her car. After she has had a long day at work, he takes her out for dinner. When he is busy doing homework for the office, she makes him a cup of coffee and some toast. When his parents are in town, she goes out of her way to make a special meal for them.

Mutual awareness

If you are not aware that your partner is allergic to cucumber, you might serve it in a salad. He or she might eat it either to please you or out of a sense of politeness, only to have an allergic reaction later in the evening. When you find out, you feel dreadful. If only you had known. Care and concern presuppose knowledge.

Knowing your partner's likes, dislikes, deep-seated fears, and unspoken aspirations help you to respond better to him or her. It will make a difference in your relationship to know that your partner is a political conservative, loves classical music, hates football, has sexual fears stemming from childhood molestations, and secretly yearns to be a landscape architect despite years of medical training. With this knowledge, you can relate to your partner as he or she IS rather than to some unrealistic image you may have formed.

In an intimate relationship, the partners endeavour to move beyond the superficial and to know each other in greater depth. They want to know how one another really thinks and feels, instead of relating at arm's length. Only in this way can they effectively respond to each other and build a realistic and close relationship.

The self-revelation needed for intimacy takes time. It may take several years before you really get to know a person well. Most people find letting down their personal defenses to be difficult. Only after you know your partner for awhile and grow to trust him or her, will you be willing to show your deepest self. Even when you trust your partner, sometimes it takes a long time before you have the courage to reveal some of your deepest fears, mistakes and aspirations.

Mutual respect

Respect for your partner is another basic characteristic of intimacy. Respect means that you see your partner as valuable and worthy of love. Unless you and your partner value each other, you will find loving one another to be difficult. For example, if a young woman does not respect a young man because of the obnoxious way he treats his parents, she will not go out with him, let alone desire to form a close relationship with him. It is hard to love, let alone like, someone you do not respect.

Respect entails accepting your partner for who he or she is. It involves not only welcoming qualities that you like, but also tolerating traits and faults that you do not like. You cannot expect to find a perfect partner who conforms to every preconceived ideal you have formed. Perfect partners exist only in fairy tales. In the real world, once the romantic haze has disappeared, you will discover that your partner has personal idiosyncracies and faults that will be annoying, even troublesome. Undoubtedly, he or she will discover the same in you. Although some of these traits, upon request, may be changed, you cannot expect your partner to change every characteristic you dislike. You will have to learn to live with your partner basically as he or she is. Not to do so, is to violate your spouse's uniqueness. To love someone ultimately means to accept that person, warts and all.

Respect for your partner also means not trying to dominate him or her. Unfortunately, this is a common problem among young couples. Many young men, despite the strides of women's liberation, still have a pronounced macho tendency and believe that men should control women, if not in all areas, at least in some. I often see young men who continually belittle their girlfriend's school achievements, career aspirations, work promotions, or arguments for not going to bed with them. They believe that only their own school achievements, career aspirations, promotions, and moral arguments count. Their conduct shows an evident lack of respect for their girlfriend's intelligence and individual development. They clearly do not accept their partner as an equal. Women who do not have enough self-respect to stand up to their boyfriends will only encourage this kind of conduct.

Of course, there are also many women who try to control their boyfriends. They push them to stop playing golf so they can spend more time together. They belittle their tastes in clothes and music, and urge them to adopt their own. Continually, they are trying to change these boyfriends and make them into something they are not. In essence, they are really unwilling to accept their partners as they are.

The failure to accept partners as they are leads to one-sided relationships. The dominant partner does not really care about the other's well-being but only sees him or her as a piece of putty to be molded. The feelings and hopes of the submissive partner are essentially ignored. True intimacy is thereby thwarted because there is no genuine understanding of each other's real desires and aspirations, and no response to one another's legitimate needs.

Mutual commitment

An intimate relationship, as we have seen, is not built in a day. It takes time for a couple to come to know each other intimately. Time is also needed to build a common life. Without a mutual commitment to stay together, an intimate union cannot occur.

To be committed to an intimate relationship means to have a strong intent to create a lasting fruitful union. The couple's initial mutual pledge to stay together needs to be continually reaffirmed throughout their relationship. Their commitment must be "for better or worse." otherwise when the going gets tough, they will not make the effort to stay together. They need to reaffirm their commitment not only in the good times when relating together is easy, but also in the bad times when it takes much greater effort to stay together.

Mutual trust

An intimate relationship requires a high degree of trust between the partners. Trust means having confidence in a person to do as he or she says. It is important in any relationship but it is particularly important in a close union. The couple need to be confident that they can rely on each other to honor their mutual commitments. They need to be secure that the other will be present in happy times as well as bad. Without trust, the partners will be unsure about their relationship and will be hesitant in giving themselves fully to it.

The intimate revelations necessary to build a close relationship also cannot occur unless the partners are confident that their mate will not betray their innermost secrets. Nothing can hurt so much as telling someone your deepest feelings and having him or her ridicule them or tell them indiscriminately to others. Mutual trust is central to a developing relationship.

Mutual willingness to sacrifice

No relationship of substance can be achieved without a willingness to sacrifice. Unless the partners are willing to give up some of their personal wants and pleasures for the sake of the relationship, a good common life cannot be achieved.

"Sacrifice" is a bad word nowadays. Most of us want to "get more out of life" rather than give up any part of it. However, rarely can anything worthwhile be achieved without sacrifice. If a young woman wants to be an Olympic swimming champion, she must be willing to spend long hours in the pool, constantly practicing her strokes. She must work with weights and control her diet as a daily regimen. Her social life will have to be curtailed or forgone completely because she will not have time to go to school or work, practice her swimming and socialize, unless, of course, she is willing to risk her future profession or athletic dream. If she truly wants to be an outstanding swimmer, she must make sacrifices. There is no other way.

Similarly, if you want a close relationship, at times you must be willing to make sacrifices. Sometimes, only small concessions are necessary, like not going to the beach because your partner prefers to go shopping at the local mall. At other times, more important sacrifices may be required. You and your partner have been saving your money for your forthcoming marriage. You want to use the money to furnish your apartment. Your partner has always dreamed of a honeymoon in Hawaii and wants to spend the money on the vacation. Since you will not have enough money to do both, one of you will have to make a major sacrifice for the other. This will not be easy.

Over the course of a relationship, both partners must show equal willingness to make sacrifices. When one partner continually gets his or her way, the relationship ceases to be a source of mutual growth and becomes a vehicle for the destructive dominance of one partner by the other. The partner who gives in all the time contributes equally to the destructiveness of the relationship. Self-sacrifice does not demand that a person give up all of his or her values and aspirations. It is not masochism. A caring relationship implies a certain give and take over time. Both parties must be willing to sacrifice for the sake of the relationship.

Mutual willingness to forgive

No relationship is perfect. As much as a couple love each other, both inevitably say and do things that offend the other. He arrives late for a special supper. She insults one of his oldest friends. They both make mean remarks during the course of an argument. If the hurt from these offenses is not alleviated, resentment will quickly grow. It is important for the offending party to apologize and be willing to make amends. However, the offended party must also be willing to forgive the transgression. Without forgiveness, continued intimacy is imperiled.

Forgiveness basically means not holding an offense against someone any longer. The slate is wiped clean. Feelings of resentment are no longer fostered and any claim for future recompense is given up. In its fullest sense, forgiveness involves making a positive effort to see the other as someone deserving of love and respect once more.

Forgiveness should not be seen as a form of self-sacrifice. It is not caving in to your partner's self-indulgent desires in order to continue the relationship, or saying "it is all right" when it really is not. You forgive your partner because you *want* to do it. Your forgiveness is rooted in *your* desire to put an end to past bitterness and resentment, and to heal the divisions that presently exist.

Forgiveness is not condoning your partner's actions. They were wrong and caused you to be hurt. Nothing has changed in that regard. What has changed is your willingness to set these past injuries aside and to work at rebuilding the relationship.

Forgiving is also not forgetting. Just because you forgive your partner's transgressions does not mean that you wipe them out of your memory. Forgiveness does not undo the past. What happened, happened. You remember the past not so you can "throw it in the face" of your partner at a future time, but to learn from the experience so that you can prevent similar problems in the future.[1]

Most of the time, the transgressions within a relationship are minor and the offending party is usually willing to apologize and make amends. In these circumstances, it is normally not too difficult to forgive. Although you have been hurt, the pain and resentment are not all consuming. Your partner's willingness to make amends are normally sufficient to make you willing to excuse the offense and get on with the relationship.

When your partner is not willing to apologize, forgiveness is more difficult. Even if the offense is minor, you will be troubled by your partner's failure to acknowledge the original hurt. Sometimes, the problem is simply a misunderstanding. You thought that your partner would meet you at eight o'clock, but he or she insists that you agreed to meet at nine. At other times, your partner may be wrong but is simply too stubborn to admit being at fault. If it is an isolated instance, it may be better to overlook the offense rather than to start an argument or hold on to negative feelings. However, if this becomes a pattern, it must be confronted. You cannot allow your partner to continue hurting you without feeling remorse or without willing to make amends. Forgiving your partner without resolving this deeper question will not help the relationship.

Sometimes, in the course of a minor argument, you and your partner may both make derogatory remarks and do some mean spirited things. Both of you may be too proud or upset to apologize or make amends. As a result, bruised feelings remain and the relationship is troubled. As long as both of you remain stubborn, resentment and anger will continue to escalate. If the relationship is to survive, one of you will have to swallow your pride and be willing to apologize and forgive the other. This will often move the other to apologize and be forgiving as well.

When an offense is grievous, the hurt and the resentment are much deeper, and even if the offending partner is contrite and tries to make amends, forgiving him or her will be extremely difficult. For example, if a young woman discovers that her boy-friend has been seeing another woman behind her back, even though he apologizes profusely and promises not to see the other woman again, her pain and loss of trust will be great. As long as these deep hurts are present, it will be difficult for her to forgive him.

In many cases, the sexual infidelity will cause her to terminate the union. Despite his entreaties, the betrayal and breach of trust will be too much for her to overcome. However, sometimes, espe-cially in a longer lasting union, she may decide that despite her pain, the value of the relationship and his willingness to make amends make trying to repair the union worthwhile. The restoration of the relationship will be possible only if she is ultimately willing to forgive him for the offense. If she continues to foster negative feelings, dwells on the need for further punishment or desires some form of revenge, the rift will not be healed and the relationship will be in jeopardy. She must stop fostering her resentment and get on with trying to restore the relationship. Even assuming that there are no further serious trangressions on his part, this will be extremely difficult and it will take time, but it must be done if the relationship is to be revitalized.

In some cases, an offense may be so grievous that you may not want to forgive the other. Although this may be understandable, in the long run, it is a mistake because you are left with an ongoing legacy of hatred and bitterness. Forgiveness is important not only because it breaks down the barriers of hurt and resentment between a couple, but also because it relieves the hatred and bitterness that exist within yourself. As long as you live in a state of resentment, nursing hurts and wanting vengeance, your whole life will be poisoned. You will not be at peace until you decide to truly forgive the other.

When I first began to teach, an administrator at the College unjustly fired one of my friends. He was unbending and would not change his mind. There was no outside recourse. I was angry and deeply resented his actions. The resentment and bitterness lasted throughout most of the year. His offensive deeds were continually replayed in my mind. Even when I tried to repress them, they seemed to find a way to return. The continuing bitter and hostile feelings colored all that I did. They surfaced in my relations with my wife and friends, and often cast a pall on our times together. My teaching was affected and so were my dealings with my children. A dark cloud hung over my life. At times, I felt physically sick. In the end, I realized that nothing was going to change his actions and that it made no sense to continue to "eat up my insides." He was not going to change, but I could. I could stop allowing his unjust actions to control my life. I could forgive his injustices and no longer harbor a grudge against him.

To forgive him at this stage did not mean that I thought his actions were right; they were decidedly wrong. Nor did it mean that the two of us could take up our relationship where it left off; the events that occurred made that impossible. I would be much more wary and distant in my future dealings with him. My forgiving him meant that what happened is over. I would no longer harbor resentment against him and would expect no apologies or amends for his actions. Life would go on.

It took me several years to reach a fuller stage of forgiveness wherein I was able to regain my respect for him. Slowly, I began to realize that he was not completely callous and unjust. He had many good points. He had quietly helped many students who were in financial need. Many of his academic decisions were beneficial in the long term for the College. I even began to see his decision to fire my friend as making sense from his perspective. I still did not agree with it, but I saw it as having more merit than I originally thought. Gradually, over time, our relations became more cordial and friendly. My forgiveness had enabled me both to have a better relationship with him and to be at peace within myself.

Mutual freedom

An intimate self-giving love relationship cannot be forced. Both partners must freely choose to love the other. You cannot make your partner love you nor can you demand that he or she love you.

Love is ultimately a free gift of the lover. You and your partner must freely choose to respond to one another. Force, coercion and demand play no part in the vocabulary of love.

Strictly speaking, love cannot be earned. You cannot oblige your partner to love you. You may be eminently worthy of love, having given much time and energy to the growth of your relationship, but your worthiness cannot make your partner love you. In justice, your partner should; but in reality, for whatever reason, he or she may no longer find you attractive. You can be ever so sweet and kind to the other, going out of your way to do special things for him or her, but your goodness and generosity by themselves cannot make your partner love you. He or she always has the choice of whether to respond lovingly to you. This is not to say that being a lovable and warm person will not normally act as an enticement for your partner to love you. It will. However, being lovable by itself does not cause your partner to love you. Love is always a free response to the personhood of the other.

An intimate relationship cannot be pressured or coerced. It exists through the free gift of the two selves to one another. That is its beauty.

The difficulties of being intimate

Although most couples strive for intimacy, it is an elusive reality for many. There are many difficulties. Part of the problem lies in the cost of closeness. To be intimate means revealing our inner selves to someone else. Many of us are not comfortable doing this. We all have dark sides that we try hard not to show, especially to those who respect and admire us. After working so hard to create a positive personal image, there seems little to be gained in telling others about our faults and weaknesses. Why risk the loss of respect or the loss of a relationship?

Being intimate means being vulnerable. When someone knows our weaknesses, they can exploit them. If I tell you some "deep dark secret" about myself, I risk the possibility that you can use it against me. What you do not know, you cannot exploit.

Although intimacy risks "loss of face" and makes us more vulnerable to others, it is the only way we have of relating to each other as we are. If I am afraid to reveal myself to you, then I will hide significant parts of myself from you. Similarly, if you are afraid of revealing your innermost self to me, then I can never really relate to you as you are. Our relationship will never get much beyond the surface level.

Developing the characteristics needed to be intimate poses another difficulty. It may sound easy to be a caring, respectful and trustworthy person or to say that we need to make sacrifices, be forgiving and be non-coercive in a relationship. However, as we are well aware, the reality is that many of us find acting in these ways on a regular and consistent basis to be difficult. On many occasions we do, but not on an ongoing basis. We are not always disposed to be loving, respectful and trustworthy persons. As a result, whether out of ignorance, weakness or maliciousness, we often fail in our interpersonal relationships.

Another difficulty is that it takes two to make a close relationship. No matter how hard we work, if our partner is unwilling or incapable of creating a close union, the relationship will not gel.

Creating an intimate relationship, then, is not easy. That is why only a minority of couples are able to establish a really close union. The ideal is difficult but far from impossible.

DISCUSSION QUESTIONS

1. Do you want a close and intimate relationship with your partner?
2. Are you afraid of being intimate?
3. How well do you know your partner?
4. Does your partner respect you? Do you respect your partner?
5. Do you find forgiving your partner to be difficult? If so, why?
6. Are you willing to make sacrifices for the sake of your relationship?
7. Are you willing to give your partner the freedom to be who he or she is?

CHAPTER FOUR

DEGREES OF INTIMACY

To my mind, the richest and most rewarding marital relationships are those where the couple achieve a high degree of intimacy and share a full common life. What makes an intimate marital union so personally rewarding is the degree to which the partners unite their lives. In no other relationship between a man and a woman does a couple become as close. Not only do they live together, eat together, and sleep together, they also share the deepest parts of themselves with each other. The two work together in the building of a common home and the raising of a family. They are present for each other in good times and bad, in sickness and health, for richer or poorer, until death finally parts them. They are friends, the best of friends.

Some of you may have reservations about using the term "friends" for a married relationship. Oftentimes, the term is used to refer to the early stages of a relationship between a man and a woman. The couple are just "friends." However, the term is also commonly used to describe a close ongoing relationship between two persons, and in this sense it is quite appropriate to refer to the relationship of two marital partners as a friendship. In a good marital relationship, the partners are usually each other's best friend. There is no one else with whom they share their existence so fully.

Having a lifelong marital friendship is a highly rewarding experience for any couple. Realistically, only a minority of couples actually achieve so close a union. Creating and maintaining an intimate relationship over a long period of time is not easy. As we have seen, intimate relating requires mutual care, respect, trust, awareness, sacrifice, and commitment. Sustaining these traits over the length of a lifelong relationship requires much patience, flexibility and tolerance on the part of the couple. Not all couples are capable of this.

Functional relationships

In fact, not every couple want an intimate marriage. Some couples are quite satisfied with a limited amount of intimacy in their marriage. They marry primarily for functional reasons, to gain status or to get out of a bad home. These marriages often last a lifetime, with only a modicum of real intimacy between the couple. The partners are usually civil towards each other and may share several common interests, but if they need or want certain kinds of personal closeness, they look for it from others.

Some functional relationships begin that way; others become that way. We have all seen marriages that start out with a romantic flourish, only to become empty shells in later years. The couple no longer desire to be intimate for many reasons: continuous bickering, an affair, drinking problems, or just a gradual drifting apart over the years. The couple stays together for the sake of the children, his job, or perhaps just out of inertia. They do what is necessary to keep the union together but share little of themselves otherwise. In front of others, they carry on the facade of a marriage, but privately, they live essentially separate lives.

A functional marriage is a marriage only in name. The couple share little of themselves. The relationship endures but the couple do not find their life together especially satisfying. Few couples today want to have such a union.

Degrees of intimacy

Even among satisfying and lasting marriages, not all achieve a high degree of intimacy. There are many reasons why this happens. Some couples are simply incapable of building a close relationship because one or both partners are unable or unwilling to be intimate for all or part of their married lives. Other couples limit their intimacy by strictly adhering to traditional roles that prevent them from sharing large aspects of their relationship. Still others restrict their closeness through a lack of common interests. All of these couples may be basically satisfied with their relationships and have no desire to separate, but their unions are not as close as they could be.

The inability to be intimate

Intimacy, as we have seen, is not easy to achieve. Many individuals feel too vulnerable to reveal themselves fully and are unwilling to disclose certain aspects of themselves. As a result, they must be content with only a limited degree of closeness in their relationship.

Rick and Joan have such a relationship. They have been married for ten years and have two children. Rick works in an auto parts factory and Joan is a part time teacher. Rick was raised in a home where he was not encouraged to express his personal feelings. Although he and Joan talk regularly about the children and the running of the home, Rick finds it hard to talk about his own persnal feelings. As a result, he rarely talks to Joan about his innermost thoughts and desires.

A few years ago, when Rick's brother contracted cancer and died within the year, the problem became exacerbated. Rick was shattered and became deeply depressed. When Joan tried to talk to him about his brother's death, he refused, simply saying that "nothing was the matter." Inwardly anguished and unable to talk with his wife about his turmoil, Rick began to avoid situations where personal discussions might take place. He spent several nights each week working as a fundraising volunteer and often went away on weekends to car rallies. Although his relationship with Joan remained amicable, progressively their union became a surface one. Joan felt frustrated with her inability to talk with him and the shallow level of their relationship, but patiently waited for him to get over his loss.

In time, Rick became more reconciled to his brother's death and his relationship with Joan improved. He did not withdraw as much and spent more time with her and the children. However, relating to her in any depth is still a problem. Even telling Joan that he loves her is difficult for him. What he cannot say with words, he does try to say with actions. He often takes her out for dinner and does many special things around the house for her. Joan knows that he cares for her, even though he will not say it. Despite the fact that she gets frustrated at times with their lack of personal intimacy, she still loves him and is content to stay in the relationship.

There are many marriages like Rick and Joan's. One or both partners have difficulty in communicating intimately. As a result, their relationship operates on a shallower basis. Critical problems are often left undiscussed, in hopes that they will go away. Sometimes they do, but most of the time they have to be resolved without adequate discussion. The couple's lack of intimacy frustrates them, but the other aspects of the relationship are good enough that they are content to stay together. Their relationship is satisfactory, even good at times, but it lacks the depth of a more intimate union.

Traditional role limits on intimacy

Intimacy can also be limited by a strict adherence to traditional male and female marital roles. Sometimes when a couple unquestioningly take on traditional roles, they assume that certain sex-related areas of their relationship are of no concern to the other and do not discuss them. As a result, significant areas of their lives remain unknown, thereby restricting their closeness. The couple will be satisfied with their limited degree of intimacy as long as they do not realize that a closer relationship between a man and a woman is possible.

Recently I attended a dinner party at a former student's home. Zoltan was married to Maria in the "old country" five years ago and they have two children. Following the customs of their families, they adhere to strict traditional male and female roles. He is the bread-winner and does the heavy chores around the house, like mowing the lawn and fixing the roof. She does the housework, the cooking, the laundry, and takes care of the children. The couple rarely discuss their respective roles with each other, except peripherally. Although both appreciate the other's efforts, their work worlds remain essentially private.

At the party, the men assembled in one room and talked about "men's affairs," and the women gathered in another and talked about "women's affairs." The dinner and its cleanup were handled by the women, and so was the care of the children. The men sat around and talked business, sports and politics. After cleaning up, the women gathered in a separate room to talk about the children, knitting patterns, and their shopping bargains. There was limited contact between the two sexes during the evening.

The party was indicative of Zoltan and Maria's relations with each other. Zoltan pursued many interests with the men of his community that he did not share to any extent with his wife. Maria, in turn, participated in many activities with her female friends that she did not share with her husband. Although the two had many common interests, like the education of their children, the overall running of the household, their families, and many personal intimacies, the male world in which he lived overlapped only to a limited degree with her female world. The extent of their intimate life together was clearly restricted by their traditional role expectations.

The marriage of Zoltan and Maria is a good one. Within the limits of their sharply defined role expectations, they relate well and are happy. It is obvious that they care for each other and their children. Yet, they feel restricted from relating more closely with each other in several areas of their lives due to the role expectations of their culture. They have been raised to believe that the male and female worlds should not mix.

Many couples from non-ethnic backgrounds also have sharply delineated role expectations that limit their personal closeness. The typical union between a "macho" male and a "Suzy Homemaker" female is a good example. He has his world and she has hers, and never the twain shall meet. If both partners are content with the bifurcation of their respective roles and the limited intimacy of the union, they will usually be satisfied with their marriage. However, if one of the partners becomes dissatisfied with these roles, the marriage will undoubtedly become troubled.

Having clear-cut marital roles does not necessarily imply that a couple cannot share their traditional male and female domains with one another. Many couples in traditional marriages do. She talks to him about his day at work and his many outside interests. He talks to her about her homemaking and child care. They are interested in each other's lifestyles, even though they do not actively participate in them. In these situations, the partners are able to override their sharp role delineation. Their distinctive male and female interests and activities are not excluded from their personal intercommunication.

Lack of common interests as limiting intimacy

No married couple share all interests in common. However, when one or both take on time consuming interests that are of little concern to the other, there is a potential for creating a marriage where the couple live in different worlds for a large part of their life together, thereby restricting their intimacy.

Over the years, I have known many couples whose sharply divergent personal interests have limited their personal intimacy. The union of Donald and Jean is a good illustration. They have been married for twenty-five years and have two children. Donald works for a manufacturing company and Jean is a secretary. They get along well together and share many common interests.

Donald, however, is a sports addict. Even though he is over fifty, he still plays softball three or four nights a week during the summer and coaches hockey three or more nights a week during the fall and winter. After the games, he usually goes out with "the boys" and spends several hours drinking and reliving past glories. When he is not actually playing or coaching, he spends hours watching sporting events, live or on television. Jean tolerates and supports his athletic interests but does not really share them. She has found other things to do while he is engaged in them. In a real sense, Jean is married to a man who has two great loves, and she is content to be one of them. The two of them are willing to have a limited common life.

There are many variations on this theme. Sometimes, one or both spouses are so engrossed in their jobs that they have only a limited amount of time for each other. Overinvolvement with volunteer work or Church activities can also restrict the period a couple spend together, as can time consuming participation in hobbies or recreational activities. Some couples are satisfied with a limited level of intimacy in their marriage; most are not.

The issue of unshared personal interests is a contentious one for many couples. Although every couple have many common interests, it is quite normal for them to have several interests they do not share. No two persons are born with the same talents nor do they have precisely the same cultural and educational backgrounds. As a result, they will inevitably have differing interests. How they deal with these differing interests can be a problem.

Two extremes must be avoided here. On the one hand, it makes no sense for a couple to be so involved with their own private interests that they neglect their common life together. In an extremely "open" marriage, where both partners are preoccupied with their own pursuits, their common life will be reduced to a minimum. A close relationship cannot be built if the couple do not make reasonable efforts to share a significant amount of their life together.

On the other hand, it also makes no sense for a couple to abandon most of their unshared personal interests in the name of togetherness. Just because she hates softball does not mean that he should have to give it up; nor should she have to give up watching "soaps" simply because he thinks they are silly. The ideal of the "closed" marriage in which the couple do everything together and nothing on their own unduly restricts each partner's individuality. The marriage will quickly become stifling because the partners will neither be able to develop their own significant personal talents nor be able to bring the fruit of their individual interests to the marriage.

Clearly, a balance is needed. The pair need to share a large number of common interests, but they also must have room to develop some of their own personal interests. The exact proportion of common interests to personal interests will vary from couple to couple, and from time to time within each relationship. There is no universal solution. Inevitably, there will be a certain amount of tension between the couple in working out these matters. Honest communication and a spirit of compromise will be needed to resolve the difficulties and find an answer satisfactory to both.

Most couples, but not all, seek a solution somewhere between a very "open" marriage and a "closed" marriage. They desire a rich common life, but they also want to be able to pursue some of their own personal interests. They are prepared both to tolerate some unshared interests in their partner and to sacrifice some of their own interests for the common good of the relationship. However, in this matter, each couple must make their own decision about what is best for them. They alone can decide how much of their lives they wish to share.

The changing levels of intimacy

In discussing the degree of intimacy between a couple, it must be remembered that marriages are always in process. They continually change and so does the level of intimacy. I have known couples who were quite close in the early years of their relationship but gradually grew apart. I have also known couples who fought for years but became very close in the twilight years of their marriage. In a good marriage, the partners usually become more intimate over time. However, even in the best of marriages, there will be dry spells when one or both will choose not to be close. Highs and lows of closeness occur throughout a marriage. Special events, like the birth of a child or a serious illness, usually draw a couple closer together, while other happenings, like arguments or job pressures, draw them apart.

Intimacy is not a quality that once attained, can never be lost. Would that it were. Relationships would be so much easier. The truth is that every couple must work daily at being intimate. What was gained in closeness yesterday must be reaffirmed and strengthened today.

Choosing to be intimate

When it comes to determining the degree of intimacy within a relationship, the partners do not actually sit down and decide how intimate they wish to be. Rather, the degree of closeness is determined both by the prior dispositions they individually bring into the union, like personal inabilities to form close relationships or strict adherence to traditional sex roles, and by the way they actually respond to various interpersonal issues that arise during their relationship. His unwillingness to talk about his job or her tendency to talk to her mother about their private affairs, will undoubtedly limit their ability to be more intimate.

Throughout a couple's relationship, whether they realize it or not, they continually make choices that will determine how close they can be. Some are content with a limited amount of intimacy, and make their choices accordingly. Others want a closer personal union and make choices that will enrich their common life. In some cases, one or both partners engage in a form of misconduct, like having an affair, that destroys the trust existing between them and makes continued intimacy difficult, if not impossible.

Summary

An intimate marital friendship is the richest and most fulfilling personal relationship that can exist between a man and a woman. It is a difficult ideal that can be attained only by a minority of couples. Some couples do not want an intimate relationship and are content with a functional union. Others simply do not have the know-how to be fully intimate. They want to be closer but have not developed the interpersonal skills to do it. Others are content with a limited degree of closeness, preferring their own specialized interests to greater intimacy with their spouse.

A lack of intimacy within a marriage does not necessarily mean that a couple will not have a satisfying union. They may. However, they could have a richer personal union if they worked on achieving a greater degree of closeness. Whether a couple's present degree of intimacy is satisfying ultimately depends on what they want out of their relationship.

DISCUSSION QUESTIONS

1. Are you satisfied with the level of intimacy in your relationship? Is your partner?
2. Do you see the roles played by husbands and wives as limited by tradition, or are you more flexible?
3. Do you and your partner share a large number of common interests?
4. What efforts do you and your partner make to create common interests?

CHAPTER FIVE

PRESUPPOSITIONS OF AN INTIMATE RELATIONSHIP: SELF-LOVE, SELF-AWARENESS AND SELF-RESPECT

Creating an ongoing intimate partnership presupposes that you and your partner are capable of building such a relationship. If either of you is not a mature person, you will have difficulty in achieving a lasting intimate union. Sooner or later, your deficiencies will surface and cause problems in your relationship. If not corrected, these traits could destroy your union.

To illustrate, if you are basically irresponsible, have little self-respect or periodically have violent temper tantrums, you will have difficulties in your relationship. No one likes to deal with a person who is unwilling to take responsibility for his or her actions, is constantly depressed or whose uncontrollable anger could lead to physical harm. If these tendencies are ongoing, it is hard to imagine anyone wanting to stay in a close relationship with you.

Self-love

To become a person capable of forming an intimate marital friendship, many personal traits and attitudes must be developed, the most crucial being a healthy love of self. Unless you can actively care for your own growth and effectively foster your own well-being, you will not realize your true human potential. Lack of concern for your own well-being will not only hinder your personal development but will also act as a major barrier in your attempt to form a close relationship with someone else.

You may be troubled by this strong and immediate emphasis on self-love, especially if you come from a religious or moral tradition that downplays human selfishness. However, there is a sharp distinction between "selfishness" and "self-love." "Selfishness" means having an excessive concern for your own well-being without regard for others. Selfish persons seek their own personal advantage at the expense of others. They are essentially narcissistic. "Self-love," in contrast, means seeing yourself as valuable and doing those things that will contribute to your personal growth and development. Self-lovers appreciate their own worth and are intent upon realizing their full human potential. However, unlike selfish persons who seek their personal goals through using others to their own advantage, self-lovers recognize that an important part of human growth entails loving others. They realize that a full personal life cannot be attained without an active and loving involvement in the lives of others.

Self-love is imperative for personal development. If you are apathetic or unwilling to make the efforts required to fulfill your own personal needs and aspirations, how can you expect to realize your full potential as a person? If you do not care about your own well-being, who will? You cannot count on others to do it for you. They may like you, even be concerned about you, but you cannot really expect others to take ultimate responsibility for your growth and development, especially if you are not interested. Ultimately, you must be the person most actively concerned about your own well-being.

To illustrate, if a young woman is a talented secretary and would like a job with a firm where she can really use her talents, she cannot sit around and wait for the phone to ring. It may happen, but she should not count on it. If she really wants to get a good position, she must take the initiative by making contacts with persons who can make "connections," doing some research and applying to several firms that offer her the best prospects. Unless she is willing to make the effort, her ambitions will be stifled.

Similarly, if a man is interested in taking out a particular woman, he must overcome his shyness and ask her for a date. He cannot expect someone else to do this. Dreaming about a date does not make it happen. Even if she says "no," at least he knows he has made an honest effort and is free to pursue another course. Loving yourself means doing those things that will enable you to fulfill your personal aspirations.

If you do not love yourself enough to seek out your own personal development, you will be dissatisfied as a person. This will inevitably cause problems in any long term relationship you have entered because you will be constantly looking to your partner to satisfy unrealized needs or to make up for your deficiencies. The problem is that any reasonable person will soon grow tired of constantly feeding your needs and propping up your ego, especially when it becomes clear that you are neither interested nor willing to help yourself.

Having a strong and healthy love of yourself is an essential prerequisite of entering into a close relationship with another person. You need to love yourself before you can have an intimate union with someone else. Love of self is not narcissistic indulgence but is characteristic of maturity.

Self-awareness

"Know thyself." This line of ancient Greek wisdom remains as true today as it was in Classical times. To love yourself and to develop as a person, you need to have a realistic understanding of yourself. Only if you have a good grasp of who you are and what you want out of life can you truly know how to care for yourself and thereby realize your full potential. Self-awareness is an essential part of personal growth and maturity.

The search for self-awareness is a common preoccupation nowadays. Knowing who you are and what you want out of life is not easy. Many questions need to be asked and carefully answered. What do you want to do with your life? What kind of career or job would you like to pursue? Do you have the ability and the qualifications to do it? Are you pursuing this line of work because you want to do it or because your parents or someone else have pushed you into it? What other interests and talents do you have? How can you lead your life so that you can best incorporate these gifts? How important are friends in your life? Do you want to get married? Why do you want to get married? What are your most important life values? Do you believe in God? What are your basic moral values? Are they really your values or are they those of your peer group or family?

To have a good knowledge of yourself, these questions, and similar ones, need to be answered. The way you respond to them will give definition to your life. Failure to come to grips with several of these key issues will mean that your life will often be without direction or meaning. As a result, you will either drift aimlessly in these areas or will allow others to direct your existence.

Adolescents are good examples of persons who do not fully know themselves. They have begun to explore their basic talents and aspirations but their lack of experience and reflection hinders them from really knowing what they want out of life. Gradually they are growing away from dependence on their parents and are beginning to form some of their own values, but they still must rely heavily on their parents and peer group for many of their values and life goals. Until they know themselves better, they will not be able to give a firm direction to their own lives.

Unfortunately, some persons seem to remain adolescents for all or most of their lives. For one reason or another, they never come to grips with what they really want out of life. Their life goals are determined by other persons or by passing whims. Their unexamined life destines them to forfeit control over the main directions of their life.

Coming to know yourself is a long term process. It takes many years of experience and reflection to evaluate realistically your underlying needs and talents, and to work out a set of basic values and goals. To complicate matters, your abilities, needs, aspirations, and weaknesses do not remain static as you progress from one stage to another in your life. Ongoing self-reflection is needed.

To reflect constructively about yourself, you periodically need time by yourself. It is difficult to think about who you are and where you are going in the midst of the hustle and bustle of everyday life. Quiet periods away from work and friends, even away from your partner, are needed so that you can think about your life, weigh your options and determine how you want to exist in the short and the long run. Without these periods of reflection, your life proceeds without direction. You do things by rote, without thinking. Instead of determining your own future, you allow passing fancies, societal pressures and personal inertia to control your life.

To marry without having a good understanding of who you are and what you want out of life can create serious problems for your marriage. A major risk is that during the marriage you may come to realize that what you really want for yourself cannot be realized in this particular relationship.

To illustrate, Helen, the daughter of a friend, married simply because it was the next "step" after high school. She had not really thought about what she wanted out of marriage or life. All her friends, it seemed, were getting married, so she got married as well. Within a year after her marriage, although she liked her husband, she began to feel trapped by the relationship without really knowing why. After some counselling and serious reflection, she realized that she had married too young and had not given herself enough time to explore other options, like travel, college or a career, all of which now had a real appeal to her. Her traditional marriage had become a trap and she wanted out. If she had a better understanding of who she was and what she wanted out of life before she married, she probably would not have married so soon. Subsequently, she left the marriage causing great pain for all concerned.

Self-awareness also requires honesty. If you are not honest with yourself about who you are and what your real abilities and deficiencies are, you will live in an unreal world of your own making. Being honest with yourself is not easy. There is always the tendency not to want to face the undesirable side of yourself, to hide from your faults and failures. From childhood onwards, you erect barriers to shelter yourself from these failings. Self-deception is often preferable to facing the truth about yourself.

It may be asked: how is it possible to deceive yourself? If you lie to someone, the deception works because the other person does not know the real truth. However, when you lie to yourself, you are a liar who knows that you are lying. If you already know that you are not telling the truth, how can you be deceived?

Self-deception is possible because you can deliberately choose to ignore certain thoughts or actions. You can, as it were, put them out of your mind and refuse to consider them. In their "absence," you begin to think and live as though they never existed, thereby creating a living falsehood in your life. In time, these denied realities can become so buried in your unconscious, that you may even forget that they ever existed.

Self-deceit can occur in many areas. For instance, you can deceive yourself into believing that your bad academic grades have nothing to do with your continual partying and poor study habits. Not wanting to blame yourself for your poor marks, you deliberately choose not to consider that possibility and put it out of mind. The bad grades are explained away as being the result of bad teachers or unfair examinations. By refusing to acknowledge the real reason for your academic troubles, you live a lie of your own making. If your refusals to face up to the real reasons for your poor grades become a pattern, you may even come to believe the lies that you have been telling yourself.

Another common example of self-deceit is refusing to acknowledge that you were the primary cause of the breakdown of a relationship. The insensitive mean-spirited remarks and the constant nagging that finally caused your partner to leave are put out of mind. Instead, you dwell on your partner's faults and depict yourself as the offended one. Refusing to look at the truth of the situation results in an ongoing self-deception. You see only what you want to see!

In both of these cases, failure to face the truth means that you live in an unreal world. Reality may be painful to accept but in the long run you are better off to face up to the difficulties now and make efforts to change your ways. The alternative is to manufacture further lies to protect your original lie and to compound the problem.

Being unwilling to face up to your real self can have significant repercussions for a relationship. Consider the case of a young woman who was sexually molested by her father during her teen years. The experience was so repulsive for her that she refuses even to think about it. She lives and acts as though it never happened. However, despite having repressed this terrible knowledge, feelings of revulsion still occur when she begins to become sexually intimate. Whenever her boyfriend tries to express physical affection, her childhood feelings are rekindled and the relationship is troubled. Because she has repressed her youthful knowledge so fully, she does not know why she has these feelings of revulsion. Resolving these difficulties will not be easy and will probably require the help of a good counsellor.

Self-awareness is not a frivolous indulgence. Without a realistic understanding of who you are and what you aspire to accomplish, you will neither be able give a clear cut direction to your own life nor to any ongoing relationship in which you involve yourself.

Self-respect

To love yourself, to want to do good things for yourself, you must see yourself as worthy of respect. Without self-respect, a genuine self-love is impossible.

A few years ago, I had a young woman in class. She was rather quiet, dressed plainly and always sat in the back of the classroom. I did not see her for a couple of years until one afternoon she unexpectedly dropped by my office. I could not help but notice the change in her. She seemed quite animated. Her hair was neatly groomed and her clothes were quite stylish. She told me that she had a problem. Recently, she had begun dating a young man who thought that she was a great person. He liked her and wanted to develop their relationship into something more permanent. She liked him and was thrilled to have such a relationship. She asked me what she should do.

Not seeing any particular problem, I was somewhat taken aback by her question. She seemed happy. He seemed happy. What was the difficulty? Her response was that she had never dated a young man who was really interested in her. All the other young men that she had dated were only interested in going to bed with her. Her parents had told her she was so ugly that no young man would go out with her except to have sex. She believed them and saw herself as having little value. She had gone out with many men but all of her dates were purely sexual affairs. Rarely did any of these men ask her out a second time.

In her conversation with me, she revealed that she had related with over a hundred men in this manner. She truly felt that she had nothing to offer them but sex. She had no respect for herself as a person. Her present problem was that she had met a young man who admired her and respected her for herself and she did not know how to handle the situation.

Her revelations to me that afternoon stunned me. Here was a young woman who for years had no real sense of self-worth. She saw herself simply as a tool to be used by others. Her parents had given her no sense of self-respect. I remember how pained I was by her story and how angry I was at her parents and those who had taken advantage of her. I also remember how grateful I was that she had met a decent young man who valued her for herself and was helping her to gain some sense of self-respect. For the first time, this young woman began to see herself as valuable and worthy of being loved. Hopefully, she would no longer allow herself to be used in such a demeaning way.

Without self-respect, you cannot realize your full potential. If you do not see yourself as essentially valuable and worthy of growth, you will not make an effort to realize your own distinctive gifts. Instead, you will either despise yourself or try to hide from the negative traits you see in yourself. In the former case, you will focus on being a loathsome person and will not want to act on your own behalf. In fact, if your self-hatred is intense enough, you may even try to destroy yourself. In the latter, you will refuse to acknowledge whole areas of yourself as being worthwhile, thereby limiting your growth potential to only a part of yourself. When significant areas of yourself are not viewed as being worthwhile, you effectively opt out of ordinary existence.

Lack of self-respect does not have to be as extreme as the case cited above to hinder mature development. Non-acceptance of one or more basic aspects of your personality can also be troublesome. For example, if you allow the fact that you are not as smart or as athletic as your brother or sister to color your perception of yourself, you may fail to see the true worth of your own strengths and abilities. The result may be that you always see yourself in the shadow of your brother or sister, and live accordingly.

Every person has their strong and weak points. You have unique talents and abilities that make you especially worthwhile. You must learn to focus on them and to develop them. You also have some weaknesses. You may not be as smart, personable or good looking as others but ultimately this is beside the point. You are who you are. You cannot be someone else. You have to play the cards that you have been dealt. To mire yourself in continual self-pity because you have been dealt a bad hand will not make things better. You must celebrate and develop the gifts that you have.

Where possible, you can make efforts to improve your problem areas. There are many ways of bettering yourself. You can study harder in school. You can learn to dress and groom yourself more effectively. You can work on your interpersonal skills. What cannot be improved, however, must ultimately be accepted.

Like all persons, at one time or another, you have probably performed actions that you now regret. You may have failed a year in school or lost a job because of your laziness or lack of effort. Under the influence of alcohol or drugs, you may have performed actions that you now deplore. Perhaps, you used other persons shamelessly for your own advantage. If it was someone close, like a boyfriend or girlfriend, you may find owning up to your actions especially painful. Whatever the case, it is important to accept that you have performed these misdeeds and to realize that your feelings of guilt and shame are natural consequences of performing actions you felt were wrong. If you are truly sorry for your misdeeds and have made an honest attempt to make amends, where possible, you can do no more. To beat your breast endlessly for your mistakes and to wallow in guilt makes no sense. You are sorry, but at some point you must get on with your life. Despite your transgressions, you must realize that you are not rotten to the core. Although your self-image may be tarnished, you are not without value. You still have the possibility to perform many worthwhile acts in the future. If repentant sinners are not worthy of respect, none of us would be respected.

Some persons are perfectionists. They tackle a task, be it writing an essay, playing a game of tennis or obeying the commands of their God, with the firm intent of not making a mistake. Deep down, they believe that they have the ability not to make any mistakes. The problem is that in trying to live up to this "unfailing" but unrealistic image of their capabilities, they will inevitably fail. Because of their perfectionist tendencies, they will have real problems accepting their faults and mistakes, and will constantly find themselves wallowing in guilt and feelings of failure. It is one thing to strive to be perfect; it is another to depict yourself unrealistically as a person who can *always* be perfect, be it in running a household or in obeying the commands of God. You are a human being and as such you will have faults and will make mistakes. Until you learn to accept your deficiencies and failures, you will value a self that you are not and can never be. Your life will be out of touch with reality.

Self-respect especially demands that you reject the efforts of parents, friends, colleagues, or partners, to demean the person that you are. Some persons take special delight in degrading others. Oftentimes, they do it simply to bolster their own insecure egos. You must stand up to these persons and not let them push you around. You have faults and make mistakes but this does not mean that you have no worth. Remind yourself that you have many fine abilities and talents. You have done many good deeds and will do more in the future. Do not let others make you think that you are worthless when you are not. Stand up for yourself. This may not always be easy but it makes more sense than wallowing in self-pity and self-contempt because you are afraid to act on your own behalf.

Lack of self-respect not only stifles self-development, it also hinders the growth of good close personal relationships. This is obvious in cases where persons have an extremely low level of self-esteem. When persons see no value in themselves, they have no desire to act on their own behalf nor do they want others to perform good acts for them. In many cases, they have no desire to relate with anyone, let alone form a close relationship.

Even when there is a partial non-acceptance of yourself, this will present problems for a relationship. For example, if you are ashamed of the fact that you came from a poor neighborhood, you will not want to talk about your early life with your partner. You may even lie about it to keep him or her from asking embarrassing questions. The problem with this approach is that you will be keeping an important part of your life under wraps. You limit your relationship with your partner by failing to show him or her a significant part of yourself.

Similarly, if you have been raised to think that your sexual nature is something dirty and debased, you will unquestionably have trouble relating sexually. Anything beyond simple kissing will make you feel supremely uncomfortable. To avoid this problem, you may limit your relationships to those that are not sexual in nature. This may solve your immediate problem but your inability to accept your basic sexuality will cause major problems when you attempt to form a more complete relationship.

Summary

Building an enduring intimate relationship presupposes that both partners have the capability to form a close relationship. Critical to the development of that capacity is the cultivation of a healthy love of self. Self-love is the active willing of a person's own well-being and growth. To love yourself is to do those things that will bring about your fullest growth and development. This includes developing loving relations with others because it is largely through loving others that you will grow and develop.

Self-love implies self-awareness and self-respect. Unless you know who you are and what you want out of life, you will not know how to care for yourself. Similarly, if you do not see yourself as valuable and worthy of respect, you will have no reason for being concerned about yourself.

DISCUSSION QUESTIONS

1. Are you a selfish person?
2. Do you have a good understanding of who you are and what you want out of your life?
3. Do you basically accept the person that you are?
4. Do you allow others to put you down or manipulate you?

CHAPTER SIX

SELF-LOVE: FURTHER REFLECTIONS

Readiness for an intimate relationship presupposes that a person has the capacity to form a close interpersonal union with someone else. Without a healthy self-love, it is especially difficult to form a close relationship. In the last chapter, we discussed the nature of self-love and two of its implied characteristics, self-awareness and self-respect. In this chapter, three further traits will be considered: personal responsibility, not being overly body-centered and openness to others.

Responsibility

To be responsible means to be accountable for your actions. It is a recognition that you are the ultimate source of your conduct and that you accept the consequences of your behavior.

Loving yourself means that you willingly take responsibility for your own growth and well-being. You do not rely primarily on others to bring about your personal development. Others may help, but ultimately you alone are answerable for your own personal growth. You are the person who gives ultimate direction to your life. You are the one who must finally accept praise or blame for the way you live.

To illustrate, if you have made a decision to go to University, you are ultimately responsible for your academic success. Aside from the exceptional case when an outside factor like illness or death in the family prevents you from realizing your scholastic ambitions, in the end you are the one responsible for your success or failure. Within the limits of your abilities, you are the one who decides how hard you want to study. You make the decision whether to stay up all night to prepare for a test or to go to bed before you finish your studying. When there is a party down the street and you have a major paper due, you determine whether to go or not. To blame your poor scholastic showing on your friends for inviting you to a party is to fail to acknowledge that you had the ability to say "no" to their invitation.

When all is said and done, you are the one who determines your academic success. Distractions of one kind or another will always be present. You decide whether to give in to them. Encouragement to study may be present from your partner, your parents or your teachers, but these persons cannot take responsibility for your actual study habits. You alone must do that. If you want to be a good student, you must take responsibility for performing those actions that will best allow you to achieve your academic goals.

In presenting this example, I am not suggesting that working hard at your studies is the only responsible approach to take at school. For a variety of reasons, you may decide that you do not wish to give full effort to your studies, knowing full well the academic consequences. Other activities, like making good personal contacts or being a successful athlete, may be more important to you. My point is that if these activities are more important to you than academics, that is your choice. However, you must answer for your priorities. You cannot blame your fraternity or your ball team for your poor scholastic grades. You are the maker of your own destiny and priorities.

Responsibility implies freedom. Human beings are free, having the capacity of self-determination. Although environmental, hereditary and historical factors limit their freedom, most adults are able to decide the basic direction of their lives. Only in extreme cases, like dire poverty or severe physical illness, is choice so limited as to be virtually non-existent.

Making choices and taking responsibility for them is not always easy. For example, when an unmarried couple conceive a baby, they are faced with several difficult questions that must be resolved. Should they get married? If they do not get married, should she keep the baby, give it up for adoption or have an abortion? These decisions will have major consequences for all involved. What they decide will greatly influence the rest of their lives.

In difficult cases, there is always the temptation to let someone else or outside events make the decisions. By so doing, the persons involved will not have to take the blame should anything go wrong.

However, if they allow others or circumstances to dictate what they should do, they forfeit the opportunity to control their own destiny. They fail to make their lives their own.

Flight from personal responsibility takes many patterns. One common form is to allow others to make major decisions for you. Although it usually makes sense to listen to the advice of teachers, parents or those close to you, in the end, you are the one who must ultimately decide your own future. You cannot allow anyone else to do it for you. To do so is to abdicate your responsibility.

If you are studying engineering at University solely because your parents are pushing you, you will surely be unhappy. If you prefer to be a history teacher, then study history courses! You may not make as much money as a teacher but, if you can live with the financial consequences, you will have the satisfaction of doing something that you want. Ultimately you must please yourself. You alone really know what you want to do with your life and therefore you must make the decisions that will help you to realize your ambitions. It might not be easy to oppose your parents' wishes, but at some point the umbilical cord must be cut.

A close friend of my sister married a young man whose parents exerted a strong influence over him. At first, his parents were fond of her, but over time they began to find numerous faults in her. They did not like the way she kept house, cooked the meals or raised the children. Her husband, caught between his parents and his wife, invariably sided with his parents. Needless to say, the marriage suffered. In time, the parents decided that their son was too good for my sister's friend and at their urging he abandoned the marriage. At age twenty-five, she was left with three young children and no husband!

Persons whose parents still make major decisions for them are poor marital risks. They do not act independently and thus there is always the danger that their parents will interfere in the marriage, inevitably causing friction. It is difficult enough to work out a good relationship with your partner without having to deal with the outside interference of parents. If you or your partner cannot act independently of parental influence, it is best not to marry. Marriage is for grownups and a person who cannot act independently of his or her parents is not a grownup. Over the years, I have never seen a successful marriage where one of the partners is still "tied to his or her mommy's apron strings."

Another form of irresponsibility occurs by consistently following the "crowd." Instead of making your own decisions, you follow your peer group out of fear of alienating them. You mold yourself in their image instead of your own.

In the Academy Award winning motion picture, *Marty,* the central character of the film regularly hangs around with a group of fellows for whom the worst crime is to go out with a woman they classify as a "dog". Marty accepts the group's values until one day he meets a charming but physically unattractive young woman. He is charmed by her and even though she is a "dog" by his peer's standards, he makes a date with her. When she arrives at the designated meeting place, he is with his friends across the street. They all make lewd remarks about her being a "dog" and he does not have the courage to go through with the date. She leaves in tears. Later, Marty realizes that he really cares for this young woman. He bolts the group and starts a relationship with her. In the end, Marty understands that he must determine his own life regardless of what his peer group thinks.

Adolescents usually are quite strongly attached to their peer group. They need to become independent of their parents but are too young and inexperienced to do so without leaning on a support group. They are reluctant to take stands differing from their friends for fear of being ostracized. Maturity gradually comes as they become progressively more willing to make decisions on their own without worrying about what their peers say.

When individuals cannot act without worrying about what their peers say, it is a sure sign that they are not sufficiently independent to be their own persons. It is also a sure sign that they are not mature enough to get married.

Lack of will power to carry out one's commitments is another common source of irresponsible actions. Some persons know what is in their best interests, but simply do not have the resolve to do so. Take the case of a young man who has worked hard to obtain an excellent position with his company. He likes his work but he also enjoys going out with his friends and drinking to all hours of the night. In the morning, he is hung over and sometimes oversleeps. His boss warns him about his repeated tardiness. He knows that his job is at stake but he is unwilling to resist staying out late with the boys. His lack of will power eventually costs him his job. He knew what was in his best interest but he allowed the pleasures of the moment to take precedence.

There are many examples of this form of irresponsibility: arriving late for a dinner engagement because you are too involved watching a televised ball game; losing your weekly paycheck in a poker game; overspending your budget because you cannot resist a bargain sale; breaking your diet because the cream puffs look so delicious. Obviously, some of these are less serious than others, but they all involve a lack of will power to carry out commitments that you know are in your best interest. They all bring immediate gratification but they do not contribute to your well-being in the long run.

All of us are irresponsible at times. We do not always act in our best interest nor in the best interests of those we love. However, when we consistently fail to keep our commitments, irritants will often be present in our relationship. If these acts of irresponsibility are serious enough, the union will be threatened. An enduring, fruitful relationship requires two responsible persons.

Preoccupation with body-centered pleasures

Persons who care about themselves are not totally preoccupied with body-centered pleasures. They enjoy physical pleasures but they see them as providing only part of their personal fulfillment, not its entirety. Their lives are open to a broader range of human activities.

For many young people, the pursuit of physical pleasure in its various forms is at the heart of their lives. This has undoubtedly been encouraged by the media. Movies, like *Porky's* and *Animal House* give the impression that high school and university students are interested only in sex and booze. Magazines like *Playboy* and *Penthouse* strongly stress the centrality of sexual pleasure in life. Ads on television and in popular magazines continually extol the virtues of the hedonist life.

There is nothing inherently wrong with enjoying physical pleasures. People have been taking delight naturally and legitimately in the pleasures of eating, drinking and sexual activity since the beginning of humankind. Difficulties occur when persons become so engrossed with pursuing physical pleasures of one form or another that they are interested in little else. Their personal development becomes arrested at the body-centered stage. The intellectual, spiritual and social sides of their being do not get developed sufficiently.

Many of us have met persons who are obsessed with sex. Their whole lives revolve around the gratification of their sexual desires. Nothing else is of any real importance. The problem with this lifestyle is that personal fulfillment is sought in too limited an area. Sexual relations cannot fully satisfy a person. If enough variety and opportunity are present, they may for a time, but eventually, like all overindulged pleasures, they will gradually lose their appeal. Sex is only one part of human life and cannot, by itself, be fully satisfying.

The movie, *9 1/2 Weeks*, provides a good illustration of the limits of a purely sexual relationship. In the film, a young woman becomes involved in a highly erotic relationship with a young man she has recently met. Sex becomes the main focus of their union. She goes along with his sexual teases, acts out his sexual fantasies, and has sex with him in unusual locations. She clearly enjoys the excitement and pleasures of his artful sexual play. However, in time, she becomes more and more uneasy with their relationship. When he insists on a triadic sexual encounter involving another woman, she realizes the hollowness of their relation and breaks it off. He, too, senses that there is problem but it is too late. Their body-centered focus prevented them from forming a deeper relationship.

A life built around alcohol is similarly limiting. In contemporary advertisements, the good life for young persons is regularly associated with drinking and partying. There is no question that many young persons find real enjoyment in this lifestyle. Getting a little "high" can be relaxing and enjoyable. The loss of inhibitions while under the influence of alcohol enables many persons to say things and to perform actions that they would not normally do. For some, getting drunk and doing silly things while intoxicated can be a source of pleasure and amusement.

The problem with a lifestyle built around hard drinking and partying is that it becomes boring and can be dangerous. Antics that were hilarious in the past become stale when they are continually repeated. Losing inhibitions is not always amusing, especially when it results in a pregnancy or the loss of a friend. Besides, there is a physical price to pay from drinking too much. Constant hangovers and the loss of mental acuteness cease to be fun. Driving while intoxicated is both dangerous and unlawful. Eventually most young people I know move beyond this stage of their life because they find it less and less satisfying. They still drink and party but in moderation. Living the "good life" of the beer commercials gives way to a better life. They find many other activities more enjoyable.

Persons who use alcohol or drugs in excess seriously limit their potential for forming close relationships with the opposite sex. In the early stages of a relationship, getting drunk may be funny or at least tolerable, but after awhile, these antics cease to amuse. What young person really enjoys a friendship where the other is continually "sloshed?" Who can take ongoing pleasure in a relationship with someone who is "hooked" on drugs?

Making sex, booze, drugs or any other physical pleasure the central focus of life puts unnecessary limits on human potential. We are more than just physical beings. To fail to develop these other areas of our personality is to arrest unduly personal development. It will also put real limits on our potential to form a deeper and enduring relationship.

Openness to others

Developing and growing as a human being cannot be accomplished simply by the pursuit and achievement of self-centered goals. Loving involvement in the lives of other people is also needed. Part of personal growth is the ability to share in the lives of others.

The loner who believes personal fulfillment can be found apart from others is gravely mistaken. All of us need a certain amount of time alone to gather our thoughts and put our lives in order, but to deliberately and consistently avoid others is to shut out the richness of human life. It puts unnecessary limits on us and blinds us to the fuller reality of our world.

Dostoyevsky's short novel, *Notes from the Underground*, tells the story of a young man estranged from those around him. He has no friends and spends most of his time alone. Because he does not relate well with others, he does not really know their thoughts or motives. Instead, he must imagine what they are thinking and what motivates them. As a result, he creates unreal scenarios about why people act the way they do, and about how he should act towards them. Needless to say, his dealings with others are strange and often unproductive.

When he meets a young prostitute who is genuinely interested in him, he cannot break out of his own world and truly share her concerns. He chooses to remain aloof and lonely. Despite her entreaties, he retreats into himself and continues to be unhappy.

Persons become loners for many reasons. Some were not loved when they were young and did not learn how to love. Others have had earlier bad experiences in relating with people, resulting in a gradual withdrawal from society. In some cases, unsympathetic family members and peers may have undermined their self-confidence making them shy and reluctant to relate with others. Whatever the cause, loners become alienated from others and their lives are solitary and incomplete.

Obsessive materialism is another reason why some persons fail to develop relationships with others. Their constant quest for money and possessions so dominates their lives that there is no room for developing real friendships.

There is no question that material things, like a new car, a fancy apartment, or fine clothes do provide real satisfaction. If they did not, why do we want them so much and expend so much energy in trying to obtain them? However, material goods by themselves cannot fully satisfy our quest for personal enrichment. To make them our central focus, while neglecting other areas of human development, creates an incomplete and unsatisfactory life. Howard

Hughes, although he was fabulously rich, became a lonely and frightened recluse, and died an unhappy man.

Possessions have a tendency to possess the possessor. We want them so much that we become obsessed with obtaining and keeping them. In the process, we lose sight of other more important values.

My wife and I got married on a shoestring. Our proudest possession was a new car, purchased (or should I say financed) shortly after our wedding. We drove it everywhere and took great delight in its possession. One snowy day in December, a colleague interrupted my class and told me that my wife had been in an accident. My first reaction was how was the car. I was pleased that my wife was unhurt, but very troubled that our car was seriously damaged. By the time I got home that night, I was horrified at my reaction. My shiny new car had become so important to me that I had lost sight of the preciousness of my wife. I had been more concerned about the welfare of my car than that of my wife. Instead of possessing my car, it now possessed me. I have never forgotten that lesson. Persons are precious; material things are replaceable.

Some people do not relate well with others because they are just too selfish. They are so concerned about their own needs and wants that they do not hesitate to use others for their own advantage. There are degrees of selfishness, ranging from performing an occasional selfish act to being selfish as a way of life. Most of us are selfish to some degree at one time or another. We act without regard for others and sometimes blatantly use them. These actions invariably cause problems in our relationships. When selfishness becomes a total lifestyle, then no real openness towards others exists. Totally selfish persons do not really care about other persons. If they do act for the well-being of another, it is only because they expect to gain from the transaction. When necessary, they will have no hesitancy in using others.

Selfish persons delude themselves. They think that by being selfish they are loving themselves in the best possible way. After all, how better to love yourself than by acting exclusively for your own sake. Other persons have value only insofar as they advance your own selfish concerns. The basic problem with this approach is that selfish persons fail to realize that total preoccupation with their own concerns prevents them from really uniting with another. They want others to do good things for them, but they do not really want to share in their lives. Effectively, this means that they shut out any real participation in the lives of others. They experience others only in a marginal or shallow way.

Most people, moreover, resent being used on a consistent basis. Eventually, they will end the relationship completely or maintain it in a distant and wary manner. If the selfish person is subtle or seductive, it may take some time for this to happen, but sooner or later it will. A self-centered person can be charming for awhile, but only for awhile.

Being able to relate with other persons in a loving way is not a frill. It is an essential part of being a mature human being. A person unable to love others is incomplete as a person.

Summary

An intimate marital union presupposes that both partners are sufficiently mature to be able to enter into the give and take of a mutual love relationship. Central to their self-development is a genuine care for their own well-being and growth. In this chapter, we have seen that caring for ourself implies taking responsibility for our own well being. We are ultimately accountable for our own growth and development. It also implies fostering the broader aspects of our personalities and not just the body-centered ones. Finally, to develop as a full human being, we need to be open to loving others. Full self-development cannot occur without real involvement in the lives of others. Loving ourselves entails loving others.

DISCUSSION QUESTIONS

1. Do your parents still make major decisions for you?
2. Do the values of your peer group dominate your life?
3. Are you willing to take responsibility for your own life?
4. Do you or your partner drink too much?
5. Are you or your partner overly reclusive?
6. Are you or your partner overly materialistic?
7. Do you always want to get your own way with your partner?

CHAPTER SEVEN

COMMUNICATION: SELF-REVELATION AND HONESTY

To build a good intimate relationship, a couple must know each other well, and this is impossible without good lines of communication. If the partners are not able to express their thoughts and feelings in a straightforward way, they will not come to understand each other. If they lack understanding, it will be difficult for them to respond to one another in a loving way. Because communication is so important for effective relating, the next three chapters will be devoted to discussing various aspects of communicating.

Verbal and non-verbal communication

Although verbal exchanges are commonly thought to be our main form of communicating, experts tell us that non-verbal communication makes up over seventy per cent of our intercommunication. We express ourselves not only with words but by our stance, gestures, scowls, smiles, and movements. The way we dress and move, the tone of our voice, and the way we act tell us much about one another.

We do not always need to talk with someone to know how he or she feels. A tired face, a glint in the eye or a firm hug often say all we need to know. Being tuned in to these non-verbal signs is an immediate form of awareness of the other.

Sometimes non-verbal messages tell us more about someone than verbal forms of communicating. All of us have had experiences with persons whose words tell us one thing but whose body language and way of speaking tell us quite another. "I'm happy to be here," he says, but his faraway look and uneasy movements send another message. In these cases of conflicting evidence, more often than not, the non-verbal communication gives the true message.

In recent years, much has been written about the importance of non-verbal communication, particularly of body language, in coming to know your partner. While it is true that being able to read your partner's non-verbal signals and body language can tell you much about him or her, it must also be remembered that often you need to talk things out to reach genuine understanding. Non-verbal signals may provide only a rudimentary indication of a more complex situation. You may know that your partner is in a "blue funk" but unless he or she tells you what is wrong, you can only guess. Non-verbal signals can be misread. You are not sure whether your partner is unhappy about something you said or did, is worried about job related matters or simply has a headache. Without some verbalization, you are unable to understand your partner's problem and are incapable of responding to him or her in a helpful way.

Non-verbal communication is especially inadequate when issues are complex. If you are troubled by your present job and are considering taking a new one in another town, this is a decision that will seriously affect both of your lives. Much reflection and careful verbal expression of your thoughts and feelings are needed to come to a mutually satisfactory decision. In the process, non-verbal signals should not be ignored, but obviously non-verbal communicating cannot take the place of a frank conversation.

For real communication to take place, the parties must not only talk to each other, they must also listen. Failure to listen is a common problem that manifests itself in many ways. He is so engrossed in the ball game on TV that he pays scant attention to her comments about her visit to her mother. Later on, she only half-heartedly listens to his complaints about his boss because she has heard them all before. Sometimes, both are so involved in their own worlds that they talk but do not really listen to each other. Their conversation is a dual monologue rather than a dialogue.

At times, all of us are not good listeners. We become temporarily preoccupied with our work or play. Perhaps we are just tired. These brief lapses usually do not pose a threat to the relationship, even though they may be annoying. However, if our failure to listen becomes a habit, a serious problem exists and must be resolved as quickly as possible. Otherwise, the breakdown in communication will inevitably lead to the drifting apart of the couple.

The importance of self-revelation

Willingness to reveal one's inner self is a key to effective communicating and achieving real intimacy. Both parties must be willing to disclose their deepest selves. They must be prepared to unveil their innermost ideas, hopes and desires, otherwise, at a certain point, their relationship will cease to grow and will remain at a more superficial level, losing the dynamic quality so necessary for love to grow.

I am sure that you have met people who are friendly and warm but at a certain point in your relationship, they are simply unwilling to give you a further glimpse into their deeper selves. You can talk with them about movies, sports, politics, and current events but you cannot relate to them on a deeper personal level. You are left wondering what they really think and feel about more personal matters. It is frustrating because your relationship never gets beyond the superficial level.

The difficulty of self-revelation

Many of us find self-revelation to be difficult. We are not always comfortable talking about our inner selves. As a result, we often limit our communication to topics that are non-threatening. Our conversations become dominated by day to day concerns that do not require much personal investment, like the latest fashions or the bad season of the Yankees.

Why is the revelation of self so hard? Why do we find communicating our deepest thoughts, even saying "I love you," so difficult? The basic answer is fear! We are afraid that if we disclose our inner feelings to our partner or anyone else, we will not be accepted or respected by them. We fear that our personal revelations will cause them to react negatively to us.

From early childhood, we have learned that unveiling our true nature can sometimes make us subject to ridicule. Little boys are mocked by their peers, and sometimes their elders, because they like to play with little girls or because they cry when they get hurt. Little girls are laughed at because they hate to wear dresses or enjoy playing football. To avoid being made fun of by others, we quickly learn to reveal our inner feelings with great hesitation even to those we love and trust. Little boys pretend they are not hurt; little girls do not let on that they really like playing football. We put up defenses and facades to cover up our socially unacceptable desires.

Unfortunately, many people have been raised in families and communities where the expression of inner feelings and thoughts has been stifled. There are numerous examples. Some of us have been brought up in homes where each time we tried to express how we really felt about some matter of importance, we were immediately corrected by our parents, and our opinions were made to appear worthless or silly. It was only a matter of time before we learned that we were better off keeping quiet. This learned behavior is often carried over into present relationships, including our closest ones.

Some of us have been brought up in families where demonstrations of affection were not encouraged. Saying "I love you" to dear ones or making public displays of affection were strongly discouraged. The result has been that expressing feelings of love for our partner or other loved ones still remains difficult. We are hesitant to say "I love you" even when we would dearly like to do so. We are ill at ease kissing or hugging our partner when others are around.

Another common problem exists for those persons raised in families that thought of sex as something dirty. Any mention of sex was always in a context of shame and secrecy, if it was talked about at all. The feeling that sex is something shameful makes revealing sexual feelings to one's partner difficult and can become the basis of future problems in sexual relationships.

Shameful past experiences are further sources of difficulty. School failures, sexual affairs or the loss of jobs because of incompetence or laziness, are events whose revelation we fear will cause us to lose respect even among our closest acquaintances. The natural tendency is to hide these experiences from others. For some of us, the sense of revulsion and guilt surrounding some of these acts is so great that we may even try to hide them from ourselves. We do not want to admit that we have done such terrible things so we simply put them out of our minds and try not to think about them anymore.

A further source of fear is our past experience of actually losing friends because of our candor. Perhaps a person we loved thought less of us because of a personal disclosure and terminated the relationship. Sometimes we ourselves could not accept our friend's revelations. Losing a friend because of our self-revelations is not a pleasant prospect, so we often stop short of revealing our deepest selves. We make the choice to have a less intimate friendship rather than risk having no friends at all. The problem with this approach, if it becomes our normal way of acting, is that we may never have any friends who will really know us in depth. None of them will really understand and respond to us as we are. Unless we are willing to risk genuine self-revelation, true intimacy is impossible.

Our communication patterns in marriage are clearly affected by these fears, whether real or imagined. We fear the loss of our partner's respect and possible rejection. We become apprehensive of revealing our innermost feelings and thoughts lest we threaten a valued relationship. Rather than risk the *status quo* which is acceptable but not altogether satisfactory, we fall back on the patterns, learned from childhood, of hiding our vulnerability and putting up defenses, thereby preventing any possibility of attaining a deeper and richer understanding.

Overcoming the fears of self-revelation

How can we overcome the fears of self-revelation? The first and best way is to take the risk that our partner will accept and respect us as we are. Unless we have the courage to risk rejection, we cannot enjoy the fruits of growing closer to our partner.

Although there is always a risk in revealing our selves, the risk is minimal when taken in a relationship of mutual trust and acceptance. When we are confident that our partner loves us enough not to use our revelations to hurt us, we feel less vulnerable. We become less fearful of showing our inner feelings and thoughts.

Trust is progressively built up in a relationship as the partners become more willing to confide in one another. Each confidence serves to encourage the partners to become more open. If you are willing to tell your partner some deeply personal feelings, this is a strong indication that you trust him or her to keep your confidences. Your implicit trust helps your partner to become more confident in telling you more about himself or herself. As more revelations are exchanged and accepted, the trust and confidence between the two of you grows, enabling both of you to be more willing to risk further revelations.

This pattern of trust and acceptance needed to enable us to feel secure in revealing our deepest selves does not and cannot develop overnight. In the early stages of a relationship, it is normal for us to be quite tentative in revealing our deeper feelings and thoughts because we do not know our partner well and do not yet feel secure in the friendship. Over time, as love and trust develop, we become more confident and willing to "let down our hair." By the time we marry, hopefully we will feel comfortable communicating in depth on a regular basis.

However, even in the closest of relationships, there will always be some things that will be difficult to disclose. Some feelings or "skeletons in the closet" may be extremely painful to reveal. We may find expressing our deep seated feelings of resentment about an abusive or unfeeling parent to be especially difficult even to someone whom we have known for years. An old "flame" returns and rekindles feelings that we thought were long buried and forgotten. We want to be open and honest to our partner but we find expressing these deep or reborn feelings difficult.

The limits of openness

Although it is important to try to communicate as openly as possible in a relationship, this does not mean that we must tell our partner everything. It is neither necessary nor possible to communicate every thought and feeling that passes through our mind. Obviously, many of our daily thoughts and emotions are hardly worth revealing. If the matter is of no great significance for the relationship, there is no pressing need to reveal it. How we feel about the neighbor's cat or shaving with cold water early in the morning might be of interest to our partner but there is no real urgency to discuss it.

However, those things that are essential to the good working of the relationship should be disclosed. If a young woman is unhappy with her boyfriend's continual moodiness, she should let him know that she is troubled by his behavior. Long term avoidance of the issue will only make the problem worse. Any disclosure that is critical to the well being of the relationship should be discussed. If there is any doubt, it is probably best to talk about it openly.

Regarding past events, the same considerations apply. It probably makes sense to mention to your partner that you have had previous relationships, but they need not be discussed in any depth, especially if you have a partner who might be unduly sensitive to these disclosures. Similarly, there is no need to discuss past misdeeds. If you have a relationship that is open, trusting and capable of handling these revelations, then the two of you may choose to discuss these matters at some length but there is no necessity. However, if something happened in a prior relationship or in other circumstances that will significantly affect your present situation or your future married life together, it should be revealed and discussed. For example, if a woman had an abortion when she was younger that might make future pregnancies risky, in fairness, she should make this known to her partner since it may affect their future married life. He should have the opportunity to decide whether he wants to risk a possible childless marriage.

A couple should try to be as open as possible particularly about matters that significantly affect their present and future life together. However, past events or present thoughts and feelings that do not affect their existing union need not be revealed unless they choose to do so.

Privacy

While stressing the importance of self-revelation and openness in a marital relationship, we must not deny the equally important need for privacy. All of us need an exclusive inner space that is free from outside intrusion where we can deal with our thoughts, feelings, fantasies, and memories in our own way. We need a private inner space where we can work through our ideas, sort out our priorities and dream our dreams. We may choose to talk about these matters, but sometimes we may prefer to keep them to ourselves, at least for a time.

As mentioned earlier, even in the closest relationships, it is not essential to reveal every thought, feeling or fantasy in our lives. Those matters that do not affect our present and future relationship need not be revealed unless we choose to reveal them. Hopefully, an attitude of openness will prevail but if we decide not to talk about certain parts of our lives, our privacy should be respected. Openness should not be forced.

In all relationships, changes continually occur. When major changes occur, it is sometimes important to think them through alone. The time spent apart clarifying our thoughts, rather than putting distance between us and our partner, should help us to be better prepared to discuss them when the time arises.

Even when matters are important, there are times when immediate self-revelation is extremely difficult. Coming to terms with your actions, coupled with the fear of losing the other's respect may cause great hesitation in revealing matters that the other should know. When this happens, hopefully the other partner will not force the issue and will respect the temporary need for privacy.

If a young man is fired because of incompetence, he may tell his girlfriend that he lost his job but he may be too embarrassed to tell her the real reasons. Since the firing will undoubtedly affect him for some time to come and may even affect his future job potential, he should tell her the real reasons as soon as he can. However, she should respect his privacy while he musters the strength to tell her what really happened. A patient and sympathetic approach is her best course at this time. Nagging will probably only make the problem worse.

Honesty

No discussion of communication can take place without some reflection on honesty. Communication is honest when it is truthful, with no intent to deceive or dissemble. In a close ongoing relationship, both partners should strive to be as honest as possible.

Since an intimate relationship is built on mutual trust, honesty in dealing with each other is essential in building this trust. Nothing can destroy trust so quickly as a deliberate lie, especially a significant one. If you tell your partner a barefaced lie and get found out, your partner naturally will lose trust in you and your relationship will be weakened. If the lie is a major one, he or she may find trusting you difficult for a long time to come.

Sometimes, persons do not actually tell lies, but they are deceitful just the same. For instance, a young man who is seeing other women while pretending to be faithful to his girlfriend acts on the assumption that "what she doesn't know, can't hurt her." However, by behaving in this way, he is blatantly dishonest and his actions are hardly loving. His life is a living lie. If the truth becomes known, the cost will be great. His partner will be badly hurt, and trust will be difficult, if not impossible, to restore.

No relationship can be close if you or your partner follow a pattern of deliberate lying or deceit. However, this does not mean that telling the truth should be done without care. Brutal honesty, simply intended to hurt your partner, has no place in a relationship. For example, a young man may tell his partner truthfully that she is not as good-looking as his previous girlfriend. If he is telling her this simply to hurt her, then his revelations are spiteful and unkind. These statements will certainly not improve his relationship. The aim of honest communication is not to "put down" your partner but to foster a close and loving relationship.

Tactfulness in telling the truth is always important. If your boyfriend puts on an outrageous combination of clothes, you know you must tell him so that he will not look foolish. But how you tell him is critical! If you tell him that he is a "colorblind idiot with no sense of taste," he will naturally be insulted and resent your comments. However, if you suggest that he looks better in another combination of colors, he will probably not be threatened and may even be thankful for the advice, provided, of course, that he has some faith in your taste.

Ideally, you and your partner should try to be as honest as possible in your relationship. However, your honesty will always be limited by your capacity to be open. The more open you are, the more you will be willing to reveal your true self. However, if your ability to disclose your inner self is limited, you will be prone to hold back the truth. Instead of being direct and honest, your defensive attitudes will lead you either to omit telling the whole truth or even to lie. These patterns of omission and lying risk destroying the foundations of trust in the relationship.

Honesty is also limited by your partner's ability to receive the truth. If your partner cannot always handle the truth, you may find being honest difficult, if not impossible. For instance, if your girlfriend is an obsessively jealous type who has fits of anger anytime you talk to another woman, you may find telling her about an innocent encounter with an old girlfriend in the supermarket to be extremely difficult. Rather than face an explosion of anger and a flurry of accusations, you may choose to remain silent. This is regrettable, but as long as she is unable to control her jealousy, you may decide that it is more prudent not to tell her about such innocent meetings.

Few of us can be totally honest in our relationships due to our own imperfections, never mind those of our partner. This does not mean that we should not try. The more we know each other, the better we can respond in love to one another. Becoming more open and honest is a process that requires constant work, but it is an effort that pays big dividends in the closeness that it achieves between the couple in the long run.

Expressing feelings

In communicating with each other, it is extremely important to disclose our feelings as well as our thoughts. Our feelings are our immediate response to the world that we perceive. Being aware of our feelings is to be aware of our firsthand reaction to the world around us. Our feelings are our direct experience of joy or sadness, of pleasure or pain. They are themselves the joy or the sadness, the pleasure or the pain. Thought can explain or rationalize these feelings but it is always once removed from their immediacy. Thinking about hurt is not to feel the actual hurt; feeling the hurt is to experience the reality of being hurt.[1]

Being aware of our feelings is to be aware of the immediate state of our life. If we are depressed or fearful, our present human situation is depressing or fearful. These feelings may result from past failures or future anxieties but they are nevertheless being felt now. Ignoring these feelings or trying to explain them away is a rejection of the actual reality of our situation.

Our feelings happen to us, whether we want them or not. They are there telling us about our present reality. To deny or suppress them is to deny what is real in our lives. For example, if a young married man gets sexually excited about a pretty young woman sitting across from him in a bar, it makes no sense for him to deny that he is having these feelings because he is a married man who very much loves his wife. In fact, he does have these feelings and he should be open to the fact that even though he is married, other women will still attract him. This does not mean that he has to act on these feelings, but for him to deny them is to deny a real part of himself.

In a close relationship, it is important that we be aware of our feelings and, where appropriate, that we express them as accurately and honestly as possible. If we are hurt by our partner's actions, we should let him or her know. Covering up our feelings or ignoring them as insignificant fails to let our partner know how we really feel. He or she cannot respond appropriately in the situation, and later may be surprised and confused by an unexpected reaction.

Obviously, it is not possible to give a "play by play" report of every passing feeling. Many are not especially significant. However, deep and enduring feelings that have a bearing on our relationship should be disclosed. If we are not open, our partner may not know how we really feel. The expression of feelings is part of genuine communication and should not be neglected in a good relationship.

The macho male and self-revelation

The way men are brought up in our society sometimes causes special problems of self-revelation. Western men are often raised not to show some of their feelings. It is not "macho" to be afraid or to be soft. Any sign of weakness or vulnerability goes against the masculine image of being strong and independent. Many of our current films and TV shows glorify this strong silent type of male. Typical examples are some of the recent roles played by Clint Eastwood and Arnold Schwarzenegger. These actors often play men who show little or no emotion. It is not that they do not have them, they just do not manifest them. They express little of their inner selves. By being quiet, they do not reveal their fears and weaknesses, making them less vulnerable to their enemies. If a man does not look afraid and does not verbally express his fears or dependence upon other persons, his rivals will see him as stronger than he is.

The problem with the "strong and silent" type of male is that he is usually a lousy lover. He is not so much a partner as a protector. He relates to the "little woman" more as a protecting parent than as a sharing partner. During the early stages of a relationship, when he is intent upon winning his partner, he is more demonstrative and is willing to express his inner feelings to the degree necessary to win her. But once the relationship becomes more solidified, he reverts back to his silent and uncommunicative ways because revealing his inner self gives him feelings of vulnerability. He feels threatened because she will come to know his weak points. Telling his girlfriend that he loves her or revealing other deep feelings are seen as signs of weakness. They show a dependence on his spouse which is not in tune with his image of the strong independent macho type. Being strong and silent may reduce his feelings of vulnerability and dependence but they also prevent him from achieving a deeper and more personal relationship.

Relating to such men is difficult. The failure of macho males to communicate means that women often do not know where they stand. When they see a distressed partner and ask "What's wrong dear?" "Nothing" is not a satisfactory answer. They may feel protected but they also feel shut out.

Helping your partner to be more self-revealing

How do you deal with a husband, or a wife for that matter, who finds revealing themselves to be difficult? There are no "surefire" techniques that can be used to help a partner to be more open. What works in one case may not work in another. Nevertheless, some basic points should be remembered in approaching the problem.

1) Create and maintain an atmosphere of trust in your relationship. If you want your partner to feel secure in revealing inner feelings, he or she must know that you will respect and honor his or her privacy. If you make a habit of telling your mother or your friends about your partner's latest revelations, it will be just a matter of time before he or she "clams up" because you cannot be trusted. Trust begets trust.

2) Be open yourself. As mentioned earlier, the best way of creating an attitude of trust in your partner is by being willing to be open yourself. Your readiness to trust your partner with your inner thoughts and secrets builds the feelings of trust needed to help him or her to be more open. Your candor will encourage your spouse's candor.

3) Encourage your partner's openness in non-threatening areas. If your partner finds being open about deeper matters to be difficult, then try talking about other areas that interest him or her.

For instance, if your boyfriend is an avid sports fan, try to get him to express his feelings to you about his favorite player or the latest game. Having his feelings considered in these non-threatening areas may give him more confidence to be open in more personal matters.

4) Be a good listener. When your partner does open up, listen to him or her. Be attentive and let your partner know that you are really interested in what is being said. Remember that what may seem trivial to you, may be very important to him or her and thus important to your relationship. If you do not seem interested, why should he or she go through the trouble, and sometimes anguish, of revealing these intimacies?

5) Be aware of your partner's body language. If your partner finds verbal expression difficult, take notice of non-verbal signals. Your mate may find saying the simple words "I love you" difficult to say, but a tender touch or glance may show you his or her feelings. Loving caresses may say more than your partner is able to say in words. Your positive response to these non-verbal signs will hopefully encourage your partner eventually to verbalize these feelings, and over time openness will increase.

6) Don't nag your partner about being open. This can only make matters worse. Continual nagging will only increase your partner's feelings of inadequacy and may make him or her "clam up" by way of reaction. When your partner does open up, positive reinforcement works much better than nagging.

Summary

Having good lines of communication is an essential part of any good relationship. If we cannot communicate our thoughts, feelings and aspirations in an open and honest way, we cannot really come to know each other. Without a good knowledge of one another, we will be unable to respond to each other's deepest needs. Communicating well is not always an easy task. In non-threatening areas, it may not be too hard to be open and honest but when it comes to highly personal matters, it can be extremely difficult. Fear of rejection may prevent us from revealing our inner selves. If we ever hope to achieve a close relationship, we must be willing to risk these revelations. A close relationship is the reward of those willing to take this risk.

DISCUSSION QUESTIONS

1. Do you feel at ease discussing important matters with your partner?
2. Are there any important matters that you are afraid to discuss with your partner?
3. How honest are you able to be in your communications?
4. In what ways has your upbringing hindered your ability to be open?
5. Are you able to discuss your feelings with your partner?
6. Can you verbalize your feelings?

CHAPTER EIGHT

COMMUNICATION: DISCUSSING MARITAL EXPECTATIONS AND PERSONAL VALUES

The time before a couple get married is the most important period for establishing the basis of their marriage. It is the time for them to come to know each other and to learn how to relate with one another. It is the period when their mutual expectations of marriage should be discussed and their compatibility for marriage determined.

As we have seen, just because a couple gets thrills up and down their spine or are turned on sexually when they see each other, does not mean that they are compatible. Romantic and sexual feelings may draw a couple together, but if the pair do not really know each other well, they risk entering a union that is not workable. The better the couple know each other and what each wants out of marriage, the better their chances of marital success.

Working out differences before marriage

Inevitably, as a couple come to know each other, they will discover that some of their marital expectations, attitudes, ideals, and values differ. Sometimes, the differences will be minor and reconcilable. In other cases, they will be large and difficult to reconcile. When the differences are sharp, the couple should not consider marriage until they have resolved them to their mutual satisfaction. *Getting married, by itself, will not solve their problems.* It may happen that the couple can work out their difficulties after marriage, but they should not count on doing so. It is better for them to postpone their marriage until they have reached a satisfactory resolution of their problems.

It is important to realize that in resolving relational differences, there is NO single right answer. Each couple must work out what is right for themselves. For example, Jim and June may resolve their differences over doing household chores by agreeing to share all jobs. Bill and Sandra may decide to follow a more traditional format. She does the inside jobs while he handles the lawn, household repairs and the car. As long as both partners are satisfied with their solution, then their answer is right for them, and that is all that counts.

There are many expectations, interests and values that a couple should discuss before they get married. We cannot mention them all, but in this chapter, several significant ones will be raised. Others will be treated more fully in succeeding chapters.

Marital expectations

All of us enter into marriage with certain expectations of what a marriage should be. These expectations come from a variety of sources: our family, our friends, the Church, the media, and our own personal thoughts. Some are the result of careful reflection. We may have watched how our parents handled money problems and vowed that we would never act in the same way. Others are simply taken for granted, like having always assumed that a marriage should have children.

Before a couple marry, it is important for them to determine if they have similar marital expectations. Do they both see marriage as a lifelong commitment that is sexually exclusive? Do they both want children? How do they expect to relate to their respective families and friends? Do they have similar views regarding male and female roles within the marriage? If their expectations are too dissimilar, they may have trouble creating a close bond.

Common interests

It is also important for the partners to determine if they have a goodly number of common interests. A couple cannot expect to share all interests, but it is important that they share many, otherwise their common life will be limited and they will continually be looking outside the marriage to satisfy some of their pursuits. The broader their base of shared interests, the fuller their life together will be.

Many mutual interests will be discovered through discussion and participation in various activities. However, common interests are not just discovered, they are often created. Some of these interests, like furnishing their apartment, flow naturally out of their developing relationship. Others can be created simply by trying out new activities together. For instance, the couple might try cross country skiing, joining a mixed chorus or taking up tennis. Some of these activities will be mutually enjoyable; others will not. The important point is to expand their fields of interest, thereby enabling them to have more to talk about and enjoy doing together.

Another way of developing common interests is by making an effort to share one or more of your partner's specific interests. You may never have gone fishing, but your boyfriend loves it. Join him a few times. You may discover that you enjoy the thrill of catching a fish or the quiet of just sitting in a boat immersed in your own thoughts. If nothing else, you may gain a better appreciation of why he is so keen on fishing.

Several years ago, while I was mowing my front lawn, a group of motorcyclists drove down the street. I was startled when one of them turned around and drove up my driveway. To my amazement, it was one of my former students, an older woman who I would never have expected to find on a motorcycle. She laughed, knowing that I would be surprised to see her on a motorcycle, and then proceeded to tell me how she got into cycling. Her husband is a keen motorcyclist. In the past, every weekend he and his friends would go out cycling and she was left at home by herself. One day she decided if you can't beat them, join them. She bought $10,000 worth of motorcycle and joined her husband on the weekends. Soon, it developed that just she and her husband would go out on a weekend. They would ride for awhile, then would stop by a stream or a roadside park and talk, sometimes for hours. Her marriage was never better. She is still not that keen on motorcycling, but she continues doing it because it has brought the two of them closer together.

Not everyone can go out and buy a motorcycle. However, her case is a good example of what can be gained when you make the effort to share some of your partner's interests.

Basic ideals and values

Most persons have certain ideals and values which are so important to them that they govern their whole way of living and acting. Religious persons base their lives on the precepts of their God. Hedonists center their lives around the pursuit of physical pleasures. Libertarians emphasize human freedom.

Usually it is not too difficult to discover these fundamental values and ideals because most persons reveal them directly or indirectly in the course of ordinary conversation. However, some individuals are more reticent. They may be afraid to express their beliefs, or perhaps their lives are in flux and they are not entirely sure what is important to them. Whatever the reason, it is important for a couple to make real efforts to communicate to each other where they stand on these important issues that are so central to their lives.

If a couple's basic ideals and values are too discordant, they will have trouble working out a strong relationship. If a young woman was brought up as a devout Christian and has been taught to treat other humans with respect and care, she may have serious problems with her ambitious boyfriend who is climbing the corporate ladder and has no scruples about how he treats others along the way. Given the disparity of their views, they will probably have difficulty finding a satisfying solution.

It is not necessary that the partners have identical ideals and values. There is plenty of room for differences. What is important is that they come to know each other's basic views on life and determine whether they can live with one another's divergent ideals and values.

Intellectual and educational values

Although intelligence is usually seen as a highly desirable asset, significant differences in intellectual ability can sometimes pose a problem for a relationship. For example, some persons would find marriage to someone who is much brighter than themselves to be intimidating and highly uncomfortable. Could you live with someone who is substantially brighter than yourself?

Differences in education can also cause difficulties. If you have a college education and your partner does not, or vice versa, would this pose future problems for your relationship? Would the non-educated partner feel inferior? Would he or she be able to share the larger intellectual world of the other? If not, would the two of you share enough other interests to have a satisfactory common life?

Career values

There are many potential issues that need to be discussed regarding jobs and careers. Now that it is usual and even necessary for both partners to work outside the home, there are several questions that directly pertain to the dual work situation. Do you both intend to work full time? As the male partner, how do you feel about your wife working full time? As the woman, do you see full time outside work as necessary for your personal fulfillment?

If you both work, how do you propose to divide the chores at home? When children come along, how will you care for them? If someone stays at home while the children are small, whose career or job will be put on hold?

Further questions arise regarding the place of work. It is not uncommon nowadays for persons to pursue careers that require them to work in different cities. Would you and your partner be willing to spend part of your married life living in separate cities so that you can actively develop your careers? If you decide not to live apart, whose career will have to be sacrificed? Will one or both of you be willing to accept lesser positions in your areas of expertise so that you can live together?

Even when a couple live and work in the same town, sometimes the very nature of the work causes problems. If your partner works for the police force or a firefighting unit, can you live with the risks involved and the hours? If your partner is a travelling salesperson who will be on the road for days, sometimes weeks, at a time, can you handle the periods of separation, especially when there are children? If your partner has a high profile business job that requires a lot of entertaining, are you prepared for it? Would you be willing to marry a doctor who is on call at all hours of the day and night? The money may be great, but could you handle the interruptions in the middle of a theatre engagement or a party? If your partner is a minister or public official, could you deal with always being on public view?

Recreational values

Work is only part of our lives. We need time to relax and to enjoy ourselves. What do you and your partner enjoy doing for recreation? Are your recreational interests compatible?

Suppose your boyfriend is an amateur rock musician and you find rock music loud and overbearing. Can you work out a relationship that neither forces him to give up his interest in music nor obliges you to listen to him and his friends? Can you at least appreciate your partner's love for rock music and take pleasure in his pleasures? Can your partner appreciate your lack of interest without feeling rejected and make efforts to share other time together?

Perhaps your idea of a fun night is to go out dancing but your partner does not like to dance, preferring to stay at home by the fire reading a book. How do you reconcile these differing interests?

Financial values

When a couple marry, unfortunately they cannot live on love alone. It costs money to rent an apartment, buy food and clothes, and make the car payment. How much money does a couple need to get married? Many factors need to be weighed: present and future revenues, savings, the cost of living in the area, and the possibility of outside help. Some couples are prepared to get married with very little money and are quite content to live frugally for several years. Others will not consider marriage until they are both secure in their jobs and have substantial savings in the bank. It is ultimately a matter of personal choice and as long as the two partners agree, either approach can work.

Once a couple have decided upon a reasonable standard of living for themselves, barring any significant changes in their revenues, it is important that they both abide by their decision and live within their means. Making a budget and sticking to it is the best way to do this.

Most couples find drawing up a budget to be relatively easy. It is basically a matter of determining revenues, expenses and financial priorities. Both partners should participate in the process so that they know where they stand financially at any given time. They should also both have a significant say about financial priorities. In those cases where the two partners find drawing up a budget to be difficult, it is probably best to seek outside assistance, whether it be a competent friend or family member, or a professional financial planner.

Although both partners should be involved in drawing up the family budget and determining financial priorities, it is usually best for one partner to handle the actual family accounting. When both parties try to do this, inevitably confusion results over whether certain bills have been paid and how much is left in the bank account. Generally, it is best for the person who is most competent in handling money to do the accounting. However, it is a good idea for the other to do the accounting occasionally so that he or she is not in the dark as to how to do them. Sickness, death or marital separation may suddenly put a person into the position of having to pay the bills and it helps to have some knowledge of how to do it.

Sticking to a budget can be difficult. It is always tempting to buy that extra pair of shoes or to decide on the spur of the moment to eat out. Although some spontaneity is always refreshing in a relationship, it is important that most of these temptations be resisted lest the couple find themselves in a financial bind. Continual overspending by one or both partners can cause many heated arguments.

In an era of readily available credit cards, it is especially tempting for a couple to buy now and pay later. Unfortunately many young couples, enticed by the ease of using a credit card and unaware of the high interest rates charged by department stores and credit card companies, often find themselves in a predicament where they can barely make their monthly payments. If one or other gets sick or loses a job, they may be in serious financial trouble. Needless to say, real care must be exercised in not overusing credit cards.

Individuals differ sharply on the issue of borrowing. Some persons pay cash for everything and refuse to have any credit cards. They do not want to risk getting into a financial bind and are content to live with less. Other persons live on the edge. They borrow as much as they can reasonably repay, so that they can enjoy the fullest number of material goods now. They are willing to risk losing these goods if their financial situation should go awry. Most persons stand somewhere in the middle. They are willing to borrow some money but are not willing to take substantial risks.

It is important for a couple to discuss how they feel about borrowing money and using credit cards. Where there are significant differences in attitudes, they may have difficulty working out a mutually acceptable approach.

Deciding on a standard of living invariably raises questions about whether both partners should work outside the home. The issue becomes particularly pressing when young children are present in the marriage. The couple must decide whether the extra material benefits to be gained by both working are worth making sacrifices in their family life. Nowadays, unfortunately, many couples do not have any real choice because they need two incomes just to make ends meet.

When both partners work, questions arise over what monies belong to the family and what monies are personal. For some couples, all of the money earned goes into a common family pool. For others, the money they earn is their own, but they make equal or proportional contributions to the family pool to cover basic family expenses. Here again, each couple must work out what is best for them.

A similar issue concerns bank accounts. Some couples operate out of a single joint checking account, taking what they need for personal expenses from this single account. Usually they will consult with each other before making any withdrawals or entries.

Other couples have a joint account for family expenses and his and hers personal accounts. Both partners keep a certain amount of money each week or month which is solely their own. This gives them a certain freedom to spend their own money without having to account for it. They can also buy presents for the other without having to take the money out of the common account. Both approaches can work well; again, it is a matter of individual preference.

It is important for a couple to think ahead to the time when they will have children and plan for the additional costs that will be encountered. Since it is common for one of the partners, usually the woman, to stay home part or full time when the child is small, there will be a significant loss of revenue. This means that the couple will have to put aside some savings for that period or will have to be prepared to live on less. A child will also entail additional expenses, like nursery equipment, food, clothes, and possibly a bigger apartment or home. These new expenses will reduce the amount of money available to buy and do other other activities. The delights of having a child will usually more than compensate for the financial sacrifices required, but at times those additional expenses and sacrifices will be keenly felt.

Differing religious values

Although our society has become progressively secular, religion still plays a major role in many people's lives. Nevertheless, in our pluralist society, it is inevitable that religious persons will meet and marry persons of different denominations or even non-believers. In fact, over fifty per cent of all marriages nowadays are between persons of differing religious beliefs. When the partners belong to significantly different religions or one is devoutly religious and the other is an adamant non-believer, the potential for serious problems in the relationship exists.

Since religious ideals and values affect a person's whole way of living, it is important for a couple having widely divergent religious beliefs to discuss their differences and to work out solutions to their problems prior to marrying. There are many contentious areas to be resolved.

The first issue to be considered is whether you can respect your partner's right to hold differing religious or non-religious views, especially if you do not find much merit in them. If you find your partner's religious beliefs untenable and feel compelled to belittle them or scoff at them, you will certainly offend your partner. It is one thing to discuss differing beliefs and to raise questions about them, it is quite another to ridicule them or to put undue pressure on the person to reject their faith or to change it. If you cannot tolerate your partner's beliefs, it is probably best to find a new partner. A person's religious beliefs are an integral part of his or her personality and cannot be rejected without rejecting the person.

If the partners belong to different religious denominations, many practical questions arise. Whose Church do they attend? Do they go their separate ways or do they agree to attend one Church together? Do they alternate Churches, going to his Church this week and hers next? Or do they simply avoid the problem altogether by not going to Church?

The differing ethical beliefs of the various denominations can also pose problems. Catholics are opposed to the use of artificial birth control, sterilization and abortion. Many Baptists oppose drinking alcohol and dancing. Jehovah's Witnesses refuse blood transfusions. Christian Scientists are opposed to taking medicines. If you are in a relationship with someone from one of these denominations, it will be important to work out beforehand how you will resolve any conflicts that might arise from these ethical beliefs.

When Catholics marry someone from a different faith or a non-believer, for their marriage to be recognized by the Catholic Church, they must promise to do all in their power to raise any children as Catholics. As a non-Catholic, could you live with that promise? Would you be resentful?

Jews are basically opposed to mixed religious marriages. They especially encourage the non-Jewish woman to convert to Judaism. Would you be willing to become a Jewish convert? If you converted, would your conversion be a true acceptance of Judaism, or would you be converting just to please your partner? If the latter, would you be able to live with the abandonment of your own religion? The same questions can be asked regarding conversion to any religion.

Perhaps the most difficult question to be resolved by an interfaith couple is how to raise their children religiously. Do you try to bring up the children in both faiths, taking them to both

Churches? In so doing, do you risk confusing your children by not giving them a firm foundation in either religion? Do you compromise and raise the children in one faith? How will you determine which faith is to be chosen? Do you try to avoid the issue by not raising the children in any religion? If you do that, do you not deprive them of basic religious values you both cherish?

Similar questions arise when one person is a believer and the other is not. Do you raise the children in the believing partner's religion or do you teach the child that religion is no longer meaningful in today's world? How do you explain the differences in your divergent beliefs?

The religious upbringing of children is a thorny issue that goes right to the core of a couple's religious differences. With respect to themselves, the couple can agree to go their own separate ways and to tolerate each other's religious beliefs. However, when a child is born, some mutual agreement has to be made regarding the child's religious upbringing and Church attendance. The problems cannot be avoided. It is probably best for the couple to try to work out these issues before marriage, lest they have serious problems resolving them after the child is born.

Mixed religious marriages can work well, but they require mutual understanding and respect of each other's positions, and a genuine willingness to compromise.

Relating with parents and in-laws

Most of us were raised within a family where we learned the basics of human living, as well as many of our values, ideals and aspirations. The influence of our parents and siblings accounts for many of our basic attitudes and ways of doing things.

In looking back, I can see how strongly my family influenced me. My mother, despite her lack of formal education, was a very thoughtful person. As a young boy, when my dad was working the night shift, I often stayed up late reflecting with her about basic human realities. My decision to study philosophy undoubtedly had its roots in those late night conversations. My father loved to play games and so do I. We spent many hours together playing cards and various board games. Together we followed the major professional sports teams and he regularly encouraged me in the sports that I played. My grandmother, the family matriarch, was a devoutly religious person. No one in the family escaped her strong religious presence and we all owe much of our grounding in Christianity to her.

Other influences were more subtle. For example, I did not realize until a few years ago that my pattern of getting angry was basically the same as my father's. When he got angry, he would storm around the household and intimidate everyone around him. I followed the same pattern for years without realizing it. After one of my blowups, my wife pointed out that I was simply following the same pattern of getting angry as my dad, a pattern that she knew I detested. I was startled to realize the similarity and ever since I have tried hard to modify my approach. As I get older, I discover more and more of these subtle influences, good and bad, that came out of my early family life.

These significant parental influences make coming to know one another's families an important premarital concern. Although my wife spoke to me often about her family in the early days of our relationship, when I first visited them, I learned much not only about them but also about her. I got a better impression of how she was raised and why certain values and ideals were so important to her.

Although our fathers were both steelworkers, the lifestyles of our families were radically different. Her family emigrated from England and brought much of the English formality with them. Nothing was ever out of place in her house. Meals were served punctiliously. The daily routine was quite constant. Having emigrated, the family lived apart from relatives and spent many quiet evenings alone reading or doing various projects around the house. My family was just the opposite. Life within my home was more casual with persons coming and going at all hours. Persons often slept late in the morning, meals were irregular and the radio or television blared most of the evening. We lived close to my mother's parents and her sisters' families in what amounted to a larger extended family. We spent considerable time at each other's homes, and every Sunday and holiday, everyone gathered at my grandparents' home to eat dinner, play games and talk about the events of the week.

Reconciling these two worlds in our married life often posed problems for us. Knowing our respective backgrounds enabled us to understand better why we often did things so differently and helped us to work through many of our divergent ways of living.

Visiting your partner in his or her familial setting can sometimes reveal traits that are not readily seen when you are alone together. For example, your boyfriend may claim to be a liberated male, but when he is at home, he may not be aware of how much his mother and sister cater to him while he sits in an easy chair drinking beer and watching television. Your girlfriend may appear to be polite and respectful, but you may be appalled by the disrespectful way she treats her parents.

It must also be remembered that the first model of what a marriage is usually comes from our family. Most of us grow up within a marital setting, allowing us to get a close look at the workings of an actual marriage. If the marriage is good, we usually try to emulate it. If it is filled with constant fighting and stress, we will usually try to build our own marriage in reaction to it. In some cases, regrettably, we may repeat the divisive patterns of our parents. If our parents have divorced, we may be more prone to see divorce as a solution to our own marital discord.

In relating with your partner's parents, it is important to know what they think about you and your ongoing relationship. Similarly, it is important to know how your parents feel about your partner. It is not uncommon for one or both sets of parents to have problems with your relationship. I would venture to say that at least fifty per cent of all couples have at least some problems reconciling their relationship with their respective parents.

There are many reasons why parents may be opposed to the union. Some parents have preconceived ideas about what kind of person they would like their son or daughter to marry, and you or your partner just do not fill the bill. Sometimes the parents have trouble with the timing of the relationship, fearing that an impending marriage may prevent their child from completing school or getting established in an occupation. In other cases, there is simply a personality clash. Of course, the difficulties may also stem from your conduct as a couple. Traditional parents, for example, will not be happy if you are living together or are obviously sexually active.

If your parents have serious reservations about your relationship, it is important to sit down and talk to them about the situation. In many cases, they will see negative traits in your partner that you do not see. They may have reasonable suggestions regarding the timing of your relationship or valid criticisms of your conduct together. Try to listen to them objectively. They are your parents and usually have your best interests at heart. It may be prudent in some cases to follow their advice.

However, it may also be true that your parents have invalid and perhaps selfish objections to your relationship. It may be necessary to take a firm stand against them. When all is said and done, it is your relationship, not theirs. You ultimately must be true to what you feel is best for you and your partner.

In some cases, it may even be necessary to break with one or both sets of parents over the relationship. Needless to say, this is a drastic step and every effort should be made to avoid it. Parents are your flesh and blood, and are an important support for your early married life. However, in some cases, you may have no choice. Try to keep the door open to a future reconciliation. Life is too short to hold endless resentments and grudges.

When a couple marry, relations with parents and in-laws do not end. Rather, the partners normally become progressively more involved with one another's family. Unless relationships are really sour, they will regularly visit and be visited by their parents, siblings and other relatives. Family birthdays, weddings, funerals, reunions, and holidays will be spent together or at least remembered by phone calls or cards. When children arrive, the proud grandparents will want to see their grandchildren regularly. During the early years of the marriage, parents may frequently help the couple financially. As the parents get older, often the couple will be called upon to assist them, even to take them into their own home. Given the continuing relationship with your parents and in-laws, it is worth making an effort to build good relations with both.

Many other questions exist regarding your relationship with your families. How often will you visit or call your parents or siblings? Where will you spend holidays like Christmas and Easter? Will you accept financial help from either set of parents? Will taking it compromise your independence? How do you deal with parents who meddle in your affairs? Can you handle their constant "advice?" How do you respond to an obnoxious parent or one who drinks too much?

Some concluding remarks

There are many issues that a couple should discuss before they consider marriage. In this chapter some of the more significant questions were raised. To most of these questions, there are no set answers. Each couple must work out their own solutions. Good lines of communication and a willingness to work through difficulties are constantly needed.

If a couple have serious differences over one or more of these issues or others, it is best that they not marry until their problems are resolved. Marriage, by itself, will not resolve their difficulties. It may happen that their problems will get resolved after they marry, but it is more likely that they will not.

DISCUSSION QUESTIONS

1. Do you and your partner have any significant problems that you have not worked out together?
2. Do you have many common interests?
3. Do the two of you share similar philosophies and values?
4. Does your partner share your intellectual interests?
5. Do the two of you have compatible recreational interests?
6. How much money will the two of you need before you are ready to get married?
7. Who will manage the family finances?
8. Will you have separate bank accounts?
9. How far are you willing to go into debt?
10. Do you share similar religious beliefs? If not, how do you propose to work out your differences?
11. Do you know much about your partner's upbringing?
12. Are your parents opposed to your union? Is it possible to reconcile your differences with them?

CHAPTER NINE

COMMUNICATION: RESOLVING CONFLICTS

It is unrealistic to think that a good relationship will have no disagreements or conflicts. The only relationship in which conflict does not exist is one where one or both of the partners are dead. Even in the best of partnerships, there will always be disagreements about basic matters. This should not be surprising. No two persons are alike. Each has his or her own particular likes, dislikes, expectations, and goals. Although a couple may agree about most matters, there will always be some disputes. These disagreements will be the regular subject of negotiation within their relationship.

The ability to resolve basic disagreements in a satisfactory way is a must for any long term relationship. If a couple do not have the ability to sit down and work out their differences, then their relationship will either be short-lived or a continual battleground.

There is no one best approach to resolving differences between partners. Some couples compromise readily. Others stand more firmly on principle. Some couples are highly demonstrative and do a lot of shouting and gesturing. Others are quieter and calmly work out their differences. Each couple must find their own way. What works well for one may not work at all for another.

Although no one approach is best, there are several guidelines that experts in the field deem to be especially helpful in trying to resolve conflicts in a satisfactory way.[1] Four that particularly deserve to be explored are:

1) Get at the issue as soon as possible;
2) Know what is troubling you;
3) Communicate your difficulties in clear terms;
4) Confront the issue and try to bring it to a satisfactory resolution.

1) Get at the issue as soon as possible

Whenever there is an area of significant conflict in a relationship, it is important that the couple work together to settle the issue in a constructive way as soon as possible. The sooner a solution can be reached, the quicker the tension and anxiety can be relieved.

If you are like most persons, you do not enjoy personal confrontations. However, if something is troubling you, it is best to get at the issue as soon as you can. To wait and hope that the problem will resolve itself is unrealistic. Occasionally this may happen, but in most cases, it will not. The best approach is to muster up your courage and confront the issue right away. If you fail to do this, the issue will continue to fester and you will remain unhappy.

Perhaps the reason you hesitate to bring up a difficulty with your partner is the strong reaction that may be engendered from him or her. Some persons, when confronted by an issue, overreact. They may get extremely angry, sulk for days or become highly defensive. Their strong reaction is intimidating, making you reluctant to bring up controversial matters in the future. These emotional pyrotechnics are their way of winning arguments even before they start. They win by intimidation. This approach is unfair and cannot be allowed to continue. If your partner will not discuss significant issues fairly, you cannot possibly build a mutually satisfying relationship. Your partner may be satisfied, but you will not be. Your ideas will never be given a reasonable hearing. This intolerable situation must be confronted and resolved before you can reasonably discuss any other problem in your relationship.

Sometimes, one of the partners stomps around in a snit for several days before getting at the problem. A young woman, for example, may stop speaking to her boyfriend for two or three days. She gives him "the silent treatment" because she feels he is spending too many nights out with the boys. Her partner knows that she is angry but he may not know why. Eventually some event breaks the ice and she is ready to sit down and talk out the issue.

Although the "silent treatment" may be a better approach than the previous one because the couple finally do sit down and discuss their troubles, it still creates needless tension and wastes time. It is best to get at an issue as soon as possible and clear the air. Silence is not always golden.

A positive technique that many couples use is to follow the old biblical adage to "never let the sun set on your anger."[2] When they have a problem, they approach each other as soon as possible and will not go to bed that night until they have resolved their difficulties. This is a commendable approach because difficulties are not allowed to linger and the couple is able to get their relationship back on track as soon as possible.

Sometimes, however, it is not practical to stay up all night trying to resolve an issue. For example, you may be furious because your boyfriend has been out drinking. However, if he is quite intoxicated, it makes more sense to wait until he has sobered up and can talk more rationally. Again, one or both of you may have to work early in the morning and cannot afford to be tired on the job. In that case, it may be best to hold over the dispute until the next day. The key point in these situations is not to let the issue drop. Arrange a time when you can further discuss the problem. If you both have busy schedules, make an appointment!

Some problems are also too complex to be resolved in one night. A satisfactory resolution will require further thought. In these cases, it is important not to let the argument linger any longer than necessary. Otherwise, the relationship will remain tense and frustrating.

A special difficulty arises for couples who dwell at a distance from each other. When a couple live in different towns or one is on the road during the week, it is not always easy for them to get at their problems right away. This means that they will have to be especially patient while waiting for an opportune time to discuss their differences.

The problems are exacerbated when the couple live at a great distance from each other. They may have neither the money nor the time to see each other for months. They will obviously have to find other means of working on their difficulties until such time as they can actually be together.

One obvious solution is to try to resolve the problem over the phone. Sometimes, this can work, but long distance telephone calls are not always satisfactory. The expense of phoning may keep you from fully talking through key points and may leave you both frustrated at the end of the call. Since you are unable to see each other, you cannot be fully aware of the other's non-verbal modes of communicating. You cannot always be sure that what is being said is to be taken as it is spoken. Sometimes, in the midst of an argument, it helps to be able to give your partner a tender touch or a hug. Contrary to Ma Bell's claims, you really cannot reach out and touch someone over the phone. Telephone calls can and do help but they cannot replace a face to face meeting. If the problem is serious, try to set up a personal encounter as soon as you can.

When you live a long way apart, writing letters may also be helpful in resolving a dispute. They allow you time to sit down and carefully state your position. However, this advantage is often counterbalanced by slow mail delivery. By the time a letter is sent and a reply is received, a week or more may have passed.

Letters can also be misinterpreted. I once had a roommate in College whose girlfriend lived five hundred miles away. They wrote daily but he often misread her letters. He would become angry and fire off a nasty letter in return. She would be hurt and reply in kind. Sometimes it took several letters, a phone call or two, and perhaps even a face to face meeting to resolve issues that arose from his misreadings. Letter writing can and does help a couple to resolve disputes but it is an imperfect instrument. Sometimes a couple must make do with the best instruments at hand.

Although it is important to resolve a conflict as soon as possible, not every setting is appropriate. For example, to raise an issue that may lead to an argument and a display of anger at a party or in a restaurant is fair neither to those present or yourselves. Public displays of crying, anger, and shouting only create a further problem. Besides the original problem, there is now the issue of "Why did you bring that up in front of all those people?" Private matters should be dealt with privately.

2) Know what is troubling you

Before bringing up an issue with your partner, it is important that you understand what is really bothering you. Sometimes, it is obvious. You are angry at your girlfriend because she was nasty to your best friend. However, in other cases, it is not so clear. Are you upset with your girlfriend because she does not find time to cook gourmet meals for you as she once did, or is the real reason the fact that her career ambitions have led her to take a job with several hours of overtime each week, resulting in less time together? Until you have thought through the matter and expressed your basic difficulty, the real issue will continue to rankle.

Sometimes, the issues are exceedingly complex and you will need time alone to determine how you really feel. For example, your boyfriend admits to you that he has been dating another woman but swears that the relationship with her is over. He wants to rebuild his relationship with you and is willing to make amends for his straying. Undoubtedly, your initial reaction to his revelations is highly emotional. You are deeply hurt. Can you get over his betrayal and start the relationship anew? Is the other dalliance really over? Can he be trusted this time? Rather than making decisions based on feelings alone, it makes more sense to spend some time apart thinking through your options. You may want to talk to friends and family. By giving yourself some time alone and consulting with others, you may come to a better understanding of how you really feel about the issues.

3) Communicate your difficulties in clear terms to your partner

Once you understand what exactly is troubling you, it is important to communicate your concerns to your partner in a clear and straightforward way. Express clearly what is really bothering you. If you hold back on the real issues, they will continue to rankle and set up the conditions for future troubles.

In bringing up your concerns, try to be specific. "You were late for supper last night. I spent several hours preparing that meal and it was spoiled. I felt frustrated and hurt. Why didn't you make a better effort to be home on time, or if you really had to be late, why didn't you call?"

Avoid the use of words like "never" and "always." It is so tempting and easy to berate your partner with phrases like "You are *always* late for supper!" "You *never* show any consideration for my efforts!" Be specific; avoid universals.

During the course of an argument, another temptation is to bring up past hurts or "old bones of contention." "Last month, I twiddled my thumbs for three hours waiting at home while you were playing cards with your cronies!" "You are just like your mother; neither of you really likes me!" Bringing up matters like these that should have been resolved in the past will only cause further pain, and keep you and your partner from resolving the existing difficulty. If a past problem has been settled, forget it. It is over and done with. Stay on the present issue. It is the existing problem that needs to be solved.

In some cases, however, bringing up "old wounds" may indicate that these issues were not really resolved in a satisfactory way in the past. If that is true, it is important to go back to these issues and to try to work out a mutually satisfying solution. If this is not done, the earlier problems will be compounded by the latter.

In most conflicts, there is anger. Anger is a natural feeling that arises when you have been hurt and in most arguments some hurt is present. In its milder form, you feel irritated or annoyed; in its stronger, you are enraged or furious. When you are angry, your ordinary reaction is to want to strike back at the object of your anger. This is a normal human emotion and you should not feel badly or guilty about being angry. How you express your anger should be your real concern.

Anger should not be hidden or kept "bottled up" within yourself. If your partner has hurt you, let him or her know that you have been hurt and are angry. The tone of your voice and your body language are good indicators, but it also helps to tell your mate that you are angry. Hiding your anger will only make you frustrated and resentful, and sets up the potential for further problems.

There are occasions, like dealing with a difficult and cantankerous boss, where you would like to explode with anger but decide that it is more prudent, in light of your financial situation, not to express your rage. However, in a developing relationship, if you are genuinely hurt and angry, your partner should be made aware of your feelings so that he or she can respond appropriately to them.

In expressing your anger to your partner, it helps to use "I" language rather than "you" language. For example, saying "I feel angry when you come home so late." is much less abrasive than "You make me so mad when you come home so late." The former expresses your feelings; the latter attaches blame. The point is to express your feelings to your partner; not to make a personal attack. You may discover, in talking through the issue, that your partner was really not at fault in the incident that provoked your ire. By using "I" language, you avoid making an accusation that will later have to be rescinded.

It is important not to overreact in expressing your anger. When you get overly incensed about small matters, your reaction is unwarranted. Instead of making an effort to control your response to these feelings, you are letting your wrath take over your life. When your partner's misdeed is small, it does not make sense to throw a tantrum. If "losing your cool" over minor matters becomes a pattern, how long do you expect your partner to put up with your juvenile reactions? You can control your reaction to these minor irritants and it is important that you do so. If the provocation is minor, "blowing your stack" is not necessary.

When the hurt is great, a stronger expression of your anger is appropriate. For example, if your boyfriend fails to show up at your birthday party because he became involved in an all night poker game, his inconsiderate act will undoubtedly provoke a strong expression of your feelings. When you next see him, you may have some strong words for him and may even yell or scream. Given the circumstance, this is not unexpected. Nevertheless, care should be taken lest you say or do something that you may later regret.

When the situation provokes strong feelings of anger, it is usually best to let off "steam" before you attempt to resolve the difficulties with your partner. Going for a walk, digging in the garden or even excusing yourself for a few minutes while you gain your composure, can prevent you from "going off the deep end" and help you to discuss matters more rationally. If you allow yourself to act when you are really angry, there is always the risk of saying or doing something regrettable. For example, triggered by your uncontrolled wrath, you may make a scathing attack on your partner's personal habits. These remarks will not be easily forgotten. Some persons are able to forget the harsh words spoken during the heat of an argument, but most cannot. To avoid the predicament, it helps to "cool down" before you confront the issue.

The point of expressing your anger is not to hurt or punish your partner but to let him or her feel the depth of your hurt. Anger needs to be expressed but it needs to be expressed in a way that will allow the two of you to understand each other better and to come together after the argument.

At no time is physical violence an appropriate way to express anger. No matter how angry you are or how wrong your partner may be, physical violence is never justified. Once you resort to physical force to get back at your partner or to win an argument, you cease to operate in a rational way and try to dominate the relationship by force and fear. Allowing your violent tendencies to override your reason demonstrates a lack of rational control expected of mature human beings.

Physical violence also creates an atmosphere of fear and anxiety in the relationship. You never know when the violence will occur again. It also risks the possibility of serious bodily harm. Injuries produced when you are angry may be regretted long afterwards. You may be able to undo anger-filled words but you cannot repair a permanent physical injury. It will remain as a living reminder of your lack of control.

Although many women slap, kick, punch, or throw things at men, studies show that males in our society more commonly use physical force against women. Greater male strength and a "macho" attitude found in some men contribute to this tendency. The "treat 'em rough" philosophy may give the "macho" male a real feeling of domination over "his" woman but if he thinks that he can get a woman to love and respect him through rough treatment, he is sadly mistaken.

If physical violence exists in your relationship, then your union is already in serious trouble. The survival of your partnership requires that the physical violence MUST STOP NOW AND MUST NEVER BE USED AGAIN. This is an absolute condition. No close relationship can be fostered in an atmosphere of fear, physical threats and abuse.

Until the violence has stopped and there is a strong commitment that it will not be repeated, the relationship should be put on hold. In some cases, it may be advisable to see a counsellor before continuing it.

Don't be fooled by a repentant attitude without a real commitment to end the violence. The typical pattern of physical abuse begins with a period of closeness, followed by an episode involving abuse and then a period of repentance by the abusive partner. The abuser asks for forgiveness and says that it will never happen again. The abused partner is forgiving and, once again, all seems well. However, the pattern soon repeats itself and continues to repeat itself as long as the abusive partner is not firmly committed to end the violence and the abused partner is unwilling or afraid to leave the relationship. The cardinal rule remains: the physical violence MUST end and there must be a firm commitment to stop it in the future, otherwise the relationship cannot continue.

4) Confront the issue and try to bring it to a satisfactory resolution

Communicating your thoughts and feelings on an issue is not the end of the process. The issue must be confronted and settled. Possible solutions to the difficulty must be determined and a real effort must be made to come to an agreement about one of them. The goal of the process is to resolve the conflict in a way that is SATISFACTORY TO BOTH PARTNERS. Sometimes, a compromise is possible. At other times, it will be necessary for one or other to give in on the issue. The main consideration is that both agree with the solution, and are willing to abide by it.

The best solution is not one where you win, or where your partner wins. It is one where you BOTH win. Both of you must feel satisfied with the resolution of the dispute. If this is not the case, then you do not really have a resolution. Sooner or later the dispute will arise again.

The major problem for most couples in resolving a conflict satisfactorily is the inability of one or both to sacrifice and make compromises. No couple will agree about everything in their relationship. Sooner or later, a clash over expectations, ideals and values will occur. When it happens, some personal desires will have to be abandoned or modified if the couple are to follow a common path. As long as one or both continually insist on their own way as opposed to a mutually agreed upon approach, a true common life cannot be created and the partnership will be in jeopardy. Building a close relationship requires both partners to be willing to give in on some matters.

"Sacrifice," for many persons, means giving up something of value without receiving anything in return. This is a basic misunderstanding of the term. "Sacrifice" is a giving up of something, but it is done with the intent of gaining a better relationship. In any good partnership, the couple must give up some of their personal desires and wants. They cannot always have their own way. However, their sacrifice is not just a giving with no receiving. They gain a shared existence that would be impossible without their mutual sacrifices. By forsaking separate paths, they forge a common union. Their SHARED existence is possible only through their willingness to make sacrifices for each other.

In resolving an issue, sometimes compromise is possible. Both parties give up something in return for a common benefit. For example, he agrees to rent a video rather than go to the movies. In turn, she consents to letting him pick the film. But when there is no middle ground and compromise is not possible, it will be necessary for one or other to make a sacrifice. If he wants to watch a Bette Midler film but she prefers to see Robin Williams, someone has to give in if they want to see a movie together.

Forgoing a movie of your choice is obviously a relatively minor matter. More serious sacrifices may be required. A young woman is offered an excellent scholarship at a College in another city. If she accepts the scholarship, she will be living a long way apart from her boyfriend. If she refuses, she will lose a first rate academic opportunity. Her partner does not want her to leave because he has no desire for a commuter relationship, nor does he want to give up his job to follow her. Will she be willing to forgo a significant scholarship to be close to him? Will he be willing to live in a commuter relationship so that she can advance in her field? One or other will have to give in since there is no middle ground. It can be a difficult decision that must be willingly accepted by both partners if the problem is truly to be resolved.

As mentioned before, over the course of a relationship, it is important that both partners show an equal willingness to make sacrifices. When one partner continually gets his or her way, the relationship ceases to grow and becomes an instrument for the destructive dominance of one partner over the other. However, for one partner to give in all the time is just as bad. Self-sacrifice is not masochism. An ongoing relationship needs a constant give and take throughout its existence.

Not every conflict will be resolved satisfactorily. Sometimes, a couple are unable to agree on an issue. Neither is willing to compromise or sacrifice with the result that the problem continues to smoulder. They fight continually about it. The continued atmosphere of conflict makes being together less and less pleasurable. In time, the ongoing battle, more than the disputed issue itself, becomes the major problem in the relationship.

I have known several couples who have had this problem. They begin by battling over an issue like whether their partner is spending enough time with them. "Friday night, you went bowling. You could have spent the night with me!" "I already spend several nights a week with you. Friday is the only night that the guys bowl. You are overly possessive!" "Me, possessive? It is more a matter of your lack of consideration for me." Because they are unable to resolve the issue, it is brought up the next time they meet, and the next, and the next. In time, the ongoing argumentative nature of their relationship destroys their desire to talk to each other or even to be together. "I hate to go out with him because all we do is fight. I like him, and I think we can make a go of it, but I am sick of the fighting!"

Few persons enjoy constant bickering. Get at an issue and work hard to find an agreeable solution. If, after a reasonable time, you cannot resolve your difficulties, rather than continually fighting about it, it may be best to separate for a period of time. Hopefully, the time apart will give both of you a better perspective on your relationship and a greater willingness to compromise. If this does not work, and no other solution is found, it may be best for the two of you to terminate your relationship.

Sometimes, a couple are not able to reach a basic agreement on an issue but they can agree to disagree. This is a form of resolution. For example, a woman may think that one of her boyfriend's best friends is an uncouth slob. She does not like his foul language nor is she happy with his slovenly dress. He, in turn, feels that despite his friend's occasional profanity and his wrinkly clothes, he is basically a nice guy. After several battles over this issue, she still views his friend as a slob and he still sees him as a good buddy. When they realize that they are not going to concur on this issue, rather than continue the argument, they agree to disagree. He still spends time with his friend but does not expect his partner to join them. She accepts his friendship and no longer nags him about it. They respect each other's right to hold a differing opinion and no longer try to convince the other of their opinion. The problem is resolved to their mutual satisfaction.

Agreeing to disagree is a satisfactory form of conflict resolution, but it does not work in all areas of discord. You can agree to disagree about your partner's friends, style of dress, political convictions, and musical tastes since these areas of conflict do not usually affect your common life together. However, whenever the clashes involve the core truths and practices of your relationship, this approach will not be satisfactory. It would be the unusual couple who could agree to disagree on the husband's sexual infidelity. Agreeing to disagree about having children, living in different towns or having a Church wedding does not make sense. These matters must be resolved one way or another because there is no middle ground.

In some cases, a couple is unable to resolve satisfactorily a dispute on a key issue. They cannot find a common ground and eventually decide to break off their relationship. This is unfortunate if it is the result of pride and stubbornness. In other cases, however, the decision to break up may be for the best, even though the couple may not fully realize it at the time. For instance, if a couple have been fighting about whether she should go back to school, they may discover through the battle that they really have different visions of what they expect their marriage to be. She sees herself as eventually having a career and working full time when they are married. He understands her career aspirations as a temporary phase and would like her to become a traditional housewife and mother. Clearly, they have differing and irreconcilable expectations about their marriage. If neither party is willing to change, it is best that they look for new partners that are more in agreement with their basic expectations.

The aftermath of a conflict

Once the conflict comes to an end, it is important for both partners to forgive the transgressions, if any, of the other. This includes the hurtful words and actions that were said and done during the argument. Human beings are imperfect and often fight imperfectly. When they are pained and angry, they do not always fight according to the "rules." These new hurts must also be forgiven. If one or both fail to forgive, then their dispute has not really been fully reconciled. Feelings of resentment and bitterness will continue to smoulder and the relationship will remain at odds. Without forgiveness, true reconciliation cannot take place.

It is not always easy to forgive, especially when your partner has deeply betrayed your trust. You are hurt and you find being responsive to your partner extremely difficult. However, to remain bitter and resentful will prevent your relationship from being truly reconciled, and will also poison your own life. Everything you do will be clouded by this bitterness. In the end, only forgiveness will alleviate these feelings and bring peace to you and your relationship. The sooner you can find it in yourself to forgive, the better.

Some final thoughts

Conflicts between you and your partner are inevitable. When they occur, get at them as soon as possible and try to reach a solution satisfying to both of you. Throughout the course of the dispute, try to relate as lovingly as possible. Even though you are hurt and angry, try to treat your partner with respect, and do not purposefully try to hurt or punish him or her. When you communicate your grievances, remember that your ultimate goal is not to put the other down, but to repair the discord existing between the two of you. Winning the argument is not important; resolving the conflict in a way satisfactory to both of you, is. You are lovers who have a problem. While working your way through the problem, keep this in mind.

Although conflicts are usually accompanied by pain and distress, if they can be resolved satisfactorily, they are a positive asset for the couple. When a couple can find a mutually agreeable solution to their difficulties, they are bound together in a stronger way. Instead of growing apart, they have grown together. They have given their relationship a new and creative direction, and have strengthened their confidence in their mutual ability to work out difficult problems between the two of them.

DISCUSSION QUESTIONS

1. How do you go about resolving your conflicts?
2. Do you get at issues right away or do you keep them to yourself?
3. How do you express your anger in a fight?
4. Do you fight fair with your partner?

CHAPTER TEN

ADAPTING TO CHANGE

All of us are a unique blend of the changing and the unchanging. Change is a fact of our existence. We are always changing and so is our partner. Within a relationship, we need to be able to adapt to these changes. We must have the flexibility to modify old ways and to incorporate what is useful from the new. At the same time, there are also unchangeable aspects of our relationship. Both of us have certain attitudes, values, ideals, and ways of doing things that will not change. Some of these traits, like honesty and trustworthiness, will be bulwarks of our union; others, like pettiness and impatience, will be disturbing and cause friction. Learning to accept and live with what we cannot change is also a necessary part of a good relationship.

Living with change

Although you and your partner undoubtedly have some basic understanding about what kind of a relationship you would like to have, your future life together is not really predictable. You can make plans, but it is important to be ready to modify them. A script cannot be laid out in advance. Larger events and happenings over which you have little or no control will bring about continual changes in your relationship. Technological advances, financial booms and busts, wars, and new social trends will shape your lives in ways that you never thought possible.

Even within your own particular situation, circumstances will arise that will force you to adjust your relationship. A job needed to finance a future marriage may suddenly be lost. The unexpected death of a parent may require the grieving partner to spend more time at home. The breakdown of a car may make seeing each other more difficult. Premarital pregnancy may necessitate an earlier marriage date.

Over the years, you and your partner will also change. Your values, ideals and dreams will evolve, sometimes subtly, sometimes dramatically, necessitating the reorientation of your union. To illustrate, a woman prior to marriage, may plan to stay at home when she has children. She feels strongly that young children need a parent at home, and since her partner has a good job, she believes it should be herself. Before the wedding, she takes a secretarial job to help provide some extra cash for the early days of their marriage. Her intention is to quit the job once their first child arrives. However, after working for a while, she becomes enthused about her position and finds that it expands her horizons. She has second thoughts about quitting work when children come along and begins to think in terms of finding a good baby-sitter or day care. Seeing the positive changes, her partner supports her desire to continue working. Their once strongly held traditional approach is replaced by a more contemporary one.

In the midst of these changes, it is important to recognize that you and your partner are not simply passive victims of outside forces and events. You are active agents in shaping your own relationship. Your concrete choices at each juncture of your union define its nature. For instance, your decisions to have children, to stop at two and to move to the country to raise them are all decisions that will define your marital union for many years to come. You are not totally at the mercy of outside forces. You are primary actors in creating the drama of your own marriage.

Even your own choices are not fixed. As time goes by, you always remain free to modify your original decisions. For instance, you can decide to have more children instead of stopping at two, and decide to move back to the city after years of living in the country. Your relationship is in process as long as you stay together.

Not all changes will be for the best. Change can draw a couple apart. It is not uncommon for a couple to break up after a significant change occurs in their relationship because one or both cannot make the adjustment. Going away to different schools, becoming overly involved with a new job, or changing philosophical or religious convictions are typical events that can cause a couple to call it quits.

I knew a young couple who had a strong relationship until she contracted a rare disease called Tourette's Syndrome. Without warning, she would suddenly start screaming or yelling obscenities. This could happen at any time or any place. Her unwanted outbursts caused her to lose her job and to become wary of going to public places. Many of the pair's times together were spoiled by her sudden outcries. She became depressed and spent many hours in tears. He became progressively frustrated. What was once a flourishing relation quickly became one filled with tension and bitterness. In the end, he could no longer handle her impromptu screams and yells, and ended the relationship. He still cared for her but he could not live with her.

Change does not have to defeat a relationship. If it does, no relationship would survive. What is needed is a continuing resolve on the part of both partners to work together when changes occur to find mutually satisfying solutions to their problems. Change can provide both an opportunity and a challenge for the couple to be together in new ways. The threat of a new situation can be turned into a fruitful experience through the couple's adaptability and love. Each time they work through an issue, they strengthen their union and gain confidence that they can make change work to their advantage in the future.

Willingness to change

Throughout the course of a relationship, there will be many times when one or both persons will have to make changes to accomodate their partner. Sometimes, this may be difficult to do, but it is important for both parties to be ready to change when the occasion calls for it. Without a willingness to be flexible, the relationship will have trouble surviving.

Why change? There are many practical reasons, but the most important reason is because you care for your partner and want to do whatever will foster your relationship. If leaving your beer bottles on the living room floor really annoys your partner, then, out of love, it makes sense to make an effort to start picking them up. If working too much overtime causes problems for your mate, then, out of love, it makes sense to try to modify your work hours. Readiness to change for the sake of your partner is a key part of any relationship. Hopefully, out of love, your partner will have a similar willingness to change if the situation warrants it.

Respecting each other's personal integrity

Readiness to change, however, must always respect a person's integrity. The partners must ultimately remain themselves in a relationship. It makes no sense for them to try to be someone they are not, just to please the other.

For example, a young woman may have a very demanding boyfriend. He is unhappy with her unisex dress style and wants her to dress in a more traditional feminine way. He presses her to wear dresses and skirts instead of jeans. He mocks her short hairdo, telling her that it is unfeminine not to have long hair. Her running shoes and sandals also come under attack. Ladies wear high heels, especially when they go out on a date. In short, he wants to overhaul her whole dress style to meet his own ideal of what a woman should look like.

For this young woman to want to change her basic way of dressing is to violate her distinctive personality. The style of dress of most persons is highly personal. They have their own taste in colors and fashion, and have specific preferences in jewelry, hairstyle and cosmetics. They see their way of dressing as uniquely expressing their personality. Although most persons are willing to receive suggestions about changing certain aspects of their dress, few are willing to modify their whole way of dressing simply to please another. They will usually see this as an invasion of their own unique way of being. They are being asked to become someone that they are not. The young woman in question is being asked to change characteristics that are distinctly expressive of her unique personality. To comply with his continuing requests is to violate her own integrity, and if she has any gumption, she should resist. He must learn to respect and live with her unique way of dressing.

In any relationship, the partners will have to learn to live with each other's basic differences and to resist the tendency to impose their own values and ideals on the other. A relationship is not a time for overhauling each other's personalities. Basic differences must be respected and tolerated.

Asking your partner to change

Despite a general willingness to accept your partner's differences, there will still be times when you will feel quite justified in asking him or her to change in some way. Some traits or actions will clearly "bug" you. Others will be troublesome because they prevent the two of you from having a better relationship. Still others will be seen as a definite threat to the well-being of your union that must be changed if the relationship is to survive.

Everyone has annoying personal quirks. When you do not deal with a person too often, you can afford to ignore these quirks. However, when you are in a close relationship, you cannot. Some of your partner's annoying personal quirks and actions will eventually "bug" you. He might belch at the table, not hang up his clothes, pick his nose constantly, or watch the television when you are trying to talk to him. She may constantly chew gum, wear saggy pantyhose, continually use the word "special," or let the dishes pile up in the sink. How do you respond to these bothersome traits?

If you are really bothered by one or more of your partner's personal quirks, it makes sense to speak up and ask him or her to change. Hopefully, out of love for you, he or she will make an effort to change. However, you cannot expect your partner to modify every little trait that annoys you. A few maybe, but not all! Perhaps, if you have a particularly tolerant mate, he or she may may be willing to make many changes. However, such a person will be exceptional.

Continually nagging your partner to change longstanding personality traits that you find annoying will quickly be met with resentment. Few persons enjoy being continually criticized for doing things that are seemingly part of their nature. "First, you didn't like my cracking my knuckles. Then, you complained about the way I dress and my occasional smoking. Now, you criticize my eating habits and the way I keep my apartment. What else don't you like about me? If I'm so bad, why do you go out with me?"

For the most part, then, to avoid continual bickering, you will have to learn to live with your partner's idiosyncrasies. The real issue is not "Why can't your partner change?" but "Why can't you learn to accept your partner's differences?" If you love your partner, as you say that you do, why can't you accept the way he or she lives?

Sometimes, you may feel very strongly that your partner's conduct is hurting the relationship and believe that a change could help. For example, a young woman may think that her boyfriend spends too much time playing squash with his friends. He is out three nights a week throughout the year. She does not object to his playing squash, but wishes he would cut down the number of nights that he is out so they can be together more.

What is a reasonable number of nights out with the boys cannot be determined absolutely. Some women are not troubled with three or four; others have difficulty with one. Each couple has to work out this problem in accord with their own expectations of the relationship. Given her unhappiness with three, it is not unreasonable for her to ask for a change. Her boyfriend's desire to play squash must be respected, but so too must her desire to spend more time with him during the summer. The couple should discuss the problem. Flexibility on both sides will be needed.

Other common examples of potentially troublesome behavior are becoming a weekend TV "couch potato" or living like a "slob" around the house. Some persons can live with these situations;

others cannot. If you are one of those who cannot, it makes sense to discuss the matter with your partner and to explore the possibility of a change. However, as mentioned before, you cannot expect your partner to change everything you find troublesome. Unless you have an incredibly pliant partner, you will have to learn to live with behavior that you may not like.

Your partner's way of expressing certain feelings can also put quite a strain on your relationship. If your mate is intensely possessive or extremely moody, you may find living with these traits troublesome at times. Under the circumstances, it makes sense to discuss your difficulties and to ask your partner to control or modify these strong responses. However, if these response patterns are deeply ingrained, your partner, even with the best of intentions, may find controlling them quite difficult. A person does not stop being stubborn or domineering overnight. Change is possible, if the person is willing, but much patience will be required on your part.

I once knew a young man who was exceptionally jealous. He would become furious and upset whenever his girlfriend spent any time with another man, no matter how innocent the relationship. His continual accusations of infidelity bothered her deeply. She complained constantly about his jealous tantrums. Despite numerous promises to change, he never really did. Knowing full well that he would probably always be a very jealous person, she still married him. Other than his periodic fits of jealousy, she found him to be a warm caring person. She was willing to live with his occasional jealous rages, although she still complains about them. Few women are as accepting. They have been married for over thirty years, and aside from his sporadic "green eyed" storms, the marriage has been a good one.

Expecting your partner to change basic values and ideals is possible, but is usually not realistic. Deeply held convictions are not easily abandoned. Normally a person will forsake them only after much thought and strong evidence that they are no longer tenable. For example, if a young woman has been raised to believe that a marriage is incomplete without children, she will not easily abandon that ideal in the face of her boyfriend's arguments that they would have more personal freedom if they remained childfree. Given her strong convictions, there is little likelihood that she will want to change, and he will have to respect her choice and be willing to modify his marital expectations accordingly. If he feels equally strong about not having children, then no compromise is likely and there may be no future for the relationship.

Your partner may sometimes do things that clearly jeopardize the continuance of your relationship. Your boyfriend or girlfriend, when angered, may get violent and physically abuse you. In this circumstance, not only is it reasonable to ask your partner to change this behavior, but it is imperative that change occur. If your partner is unwilling to make a firm commitment to stop being violent, it makes sense to terminate the relationship.

In this whole discussion of asking your partner to change, a basic point to be remembered is that you cannot change your partner. *He or she must do that.* You can ask, plead or cajole, but ultimately the other must make the decision to change. If he or she is unwilling to change, then you will have to decide if the relationship is worth continuing. If it is, then you will have to learn to accept your partner's annoying traits or troublesome behavior. That is all you really can do. Continuous nagging will only cause further problems. If your partner's conduct and attitudes deeply trouble you, then you should probably stop seeing each other.

Some concluding thoughts

A relationship is a dynamic entity. Change, wanted or unwanted, is always occurring. Sometimes, it is an outside event that forces the change. At other times, it is a change in the values, ideals, or conduct of the partners. In dealing with change, the couple need to be flexible. They must be willing to bend on occasion, and not always stand on principle. They need to be willing to compromise or even to sacrifice significant desires. However, sometimes, it is important for their personal integrity to stand on principle or to refuse to change longstanding traits or idiosyncrasies. In these situations, the other partner will have to learn to accept and live with these differences and foibles.

In the best of relationships, the partners are committed to their union and will make every effort to work through any difficulties. They are resolved not to let change or the lack of change defeat their union. They will not give up when the going gets rough. To paraphrase the prayer of St. Francis, they have the courage to change what needs to be changed, the patience to accept what cannot be changed, and the wisdom to distinguish one from the other.

DISCUSSION QUESTIONS

1. Are there aspects of your relationship that you think should be changed? If so, have you discussed them with your partner?
2. Are you afraid of change?
3. Do you feel that you need to change in any way before you get married?
4. Does your partner respect your personal integrity? Do you respect your partner's?
5. Can you accept your partner's faults? Does your partner accept yours?

CHAPTER ELEVEN

COMMITMENT

Much is said and written about the importance of commitment in discussion of relationships nowadays. This concern is well justified because without a firm mutual commitment, a lasting marital friendship is virtually impossible. Since a close relationship takes time to develop and requires continuing togetherness, a couple need to be able to give each other clear assurances that they will remain together and will work at their relationship.

What is a commitment?

In its most basic meaning, a commitment is a pledge or a strong promise to do or forswear something in the future. It is a personal statement that you will make a serious effort to act in a particular way now and in the time to come. A commitment can be self-directed, as when you commit yourself to improving your grades in the next school term, or it can be other-directed, as when you promise to pay off your bank loan in the next year. Commitments can be temporary or permanent; they may or may not have legal implications. Often they are verbalized, sometimes they are written down and in some cases they are understood but left unspoken.

When a commitment is made to another person, it gives him or her reason to expect the performance or forbearance of a specified act. When I promise my son to take him to a basketball game, he can rightfully expect that I will make a reasonable effort to take him. I have given him my word that I will. "To give my word" means that I will make a serious attempt to take him. I have singled out this action as being truly important for us both. If I do not make a reasonable effort to fulfill my promise, I will feel troubled or ashamed, and he will feel disappointed or hurt.

There are varying degrees of commitment in a typical developing relationship. When the couple first start dating, there is very little commitment to each other. They see each other on a regular basis, but they do not rule out dates with other persons. The relationship is not seen yet as anything other than a casual friendship. In time, as the friendship grows, the couple make a deeper commitment. They spend more time together and do not date others. They are mutually happy in their closer bond, but the door is still open should one or both decide to leave. If and when the couple become engaged, they make a strong mutual commitment to build a life together. They are resolved to make every effort to create a permanent relationship and will break up at this stage only if a truly serious problem cannot be reconciled. At each point along the way, commitment is present, but it becomes stronger as the couple are more firmly resolved to make their friendship into a permanent and exclusive union.

Marriage as a permanent commitment

Marriage is a permanent commitment. It is a lifelong exclusive union. Few couples have any sympathy with the idea of marriage as a temporary union. Only the rare couple is interested in a five year renewable contract.

Most marriage vows include a line like "until death do us part" to indicate the permanence of the vows made. However, this phrase has become ambiguous in recent years. In the past, when couples vowed to remain together until death, they literally understood their union as lasting until the death of one of the partners. If serious problems arose in their marriage and there was no possibility of reconciliation, they would either tough it out in some type of functional union or separate without any thought of remarrying. Past religious and civil laws clearly sanctioned this approach to marriage.

Many persons still view their marriages in this way, but in recent years, attitudes have changed. Most people still want a permanent marital union, but if there are serious problems in their relationship, like repeated infidelities or physical abuse, then they will terminate their union, perhaps reluctantly. For these persons, "until death do us part" means until the death of the relationship, not simply physical death. Once they see no possibility of reconciliation, they will no longer consider themselves married. They intend a permanent union and will make every effort to make it succeed, but if, despite all their best efforts, the marriage irretrievably breaks down, they see themselves as free to marry another. Some couples have purposely taken the phrase "until death do us part" out of their marital vows and substituted lines like "until our relationship dies" or "until our love ends" to better express their real intent.

In both attitudes, the partners are strongly committed to a permanent relationship. They do not want a temporary union nor are they looking for an easy way out of their marriage. The point at issue is the question of what happens should the marriage actually break down. The traditional model is "once married, always married." Even though your partner deserts you, beats you, flagrantly commits adultery, or remarries, you are still married. You may lead separate lives, but you cannot remarry unless your partner dies. The more recent model is that once the marriage is irretrievably broken down, the marriage is over. Every reasonable effort should be made to save the marriage but when it becomes clear that it is no longer possible for the couple to live together as husband and wife, they are no longer bound to each other. They intended a permanent union, but the realities of their lives prevented them from realizing the promises they made in all sincerity.

Traditionalists argue that once the door is open for ending a marriage, abuse of this right will follow. One or both of the partners will be more willing to give up on a troubled marriage rather than trying to rebuild it. Contemporaries respond that the traditional view leads to persons being forced to stay in bad relationships, causing needless suffering to all involved. It also brings about the existence of long term separations for persons who may badly want and need the love and companionship of a marriage.

In the end, you and your partner, in the light of your own personal, familial and religious beliefs, will have to determine how you understand the permanence of your commitment. Does your intent to have a permanent union mean that you consider yourself bound to your partner until one of you dies? Does it allow for remarriage in the event of irreparable marriage breakdown? Hopefully, your union will never reach the state where a final resolution of this problem will have to be made.

Why make a permanent commitment?

At a time when marriage breakdown is so prevalent, why would you want to make a permanent commitment to your partner?

When you reflect about the future, with all its unforeseen possibilities, binding yourself to the same person every day of your life is a scary thought. The rest of your life could be fifty years or more!

We make very few permanent commitments to other persons during our lifetimes. Marriage is perhaps the most obvious but there are other important ones. We make lifelong commitments to our parents, our children and special friends. When they need us, we are there to help.

We make these commitments for many reasons: status, money, a sense of duty, or a need for security. But, without question, the best reason to make a permanent commitment is LOVE. It is because we *love* our partner, our parents, our children, and our friends that we want to be there for them and with them for the rest of our lives. When we love others deeply, we want to be with them, as the old song goes, "not for just a day, not for just a year, but always." We cannot imagine life apart from them.

Most young people want to get married primarily because they love each other. When my wife and I talk to couples preparing for marriage, it becomes quickly apparent that their love is so great that they can't bear the thought of ever being apart. Making a permanent commitment is not viewed as being a "ball and chain" but flows naturally from their loving relationship.

How could it be otherwise? Could you imagine staying in an intimate relationship where you did not love your partner or your partner did not love you? Would you be content to stay together just for the sake of the children, your parents or your community image? Would you be willing to get married simply because it is your duty? If a premarital pregnancy occurred in your relationship and you felt pressured to marry, would you find marrying under these pressures satisfying? If you did not love your partner, no matter how honorable your action, could you be fully content in the marriage?

The point in being married is not just to stay together for the rest of your lives. Marriage is not an endurance contest. Rather, the partners want to create an ongoing bond of love that is rewarding for both of them. They want permanence because they love each other. Permanence flows from love, not love from permanence!

Some advantages of a long term commitment

Aside from the obvious benefit of having a lifelong friend and companion, making an exclusive long term commitment has many other attendant benefits. When the partners make a vow to stay together, they assure each other that they are both going to work hard to foster their union. Continued assurances and demonstrations of serious intent throughout the relationship builds confidence in each other's promises and their ability to honor them, giving the couple a growing sense of security in their relationship.

A long term marital commitment allows a couple to plan their distant future together more easily and realistically. Without this commitment, making long range plans is difficult. As long as a couple are not sure of their future together, they will be reluctant to make such plans.

Couples who live together in an open-ended arrangement, where both parties are free to leave at any time, have this problem. They may love each other and are committed to working at their relationship but they are not interested in a permanent bond at this stage in their lives. As a result, they have difficulty planning their long term future. For example, the partners may be reluctant to have a child because they may not be together in the time to come. They may be hesitant to buy a house or make any other major investment together for the same reason. Some cohabiting couples make a point throughout their relationship of carefully distinguishing between who owns what in case of a future breakup. The lack of a permanent commitment clearly puts serious limits on their ability to share their future.

A lifelong marital commitment also gives a couple the time needed to grow into a relationship. Prior to marriage, there is a period of give and take whereby the partners learn to live together in a fruitful way. After marrying, of course, this process does not end. There is more to learn about each other, projects to be continued and new satisfactions to be discovered. It takes time for many of these good things to be brought to fruition. As well, faults remain, mistakes continue to be made and new problems arise. The resolution of many of these difficulties will not happen overnight. A long term marital commitment is a mutual statement by the partners that they are willing to give their relationship the time to realize its potential benefits and to work through any problems.

Rushing a marital commitment

Needless to say, making a marital commitment is an extremely serious decision. It binds you in a close relationship for the rest of your life and strongly affects the lives of your partner and any future children you may have. Unless you are ready to take on the responsibilities implied in getting married, it makes no sense to get married. Rushing into a marriage risks unnecessary hurt for yourself, your partner and your future family.

Although divorce is always a possibility, knowing you have an "escape clause" should not be a factor in your decision to get married. It makes no sense to make a permanent commitment when you are still concerned about how you can get out of it. If you have serious reservations about making a lifelong commitment, then you should not get married. It is better to wait until all of your major reservations are gone.

If you feel that you are ready and your partner does not, it does not make sense to push him or her into making a marital commitment. Statements like: "If you really loved me, you would marry me!" or "If you were a real man, you wouldn't be afraid to make a commitment!" are unfair. You must give your partner the freedom to make his or her own decision. Psychological coercion may bring about a marriage, but it will only create an unwilling partner who will eventually release pent up resentment with disastrous results for the marriage. A forced relationship will only threaten the very love that you seek to attain.

The temptation to rush into marriage comes from many quarters. As mentioned before, the lure of romance and/or sexual passion can often seduce a young couple into making a marital commitment before they really know each other. The fear of being "left behind" also entices some lonely persons to rush into a marriage that is ill conceived.

The glamour and romance of a wedding itself can act as a real temptation for some persons, especially younger women, to get married sooner than they should. The glamour of being queen for a day, picking bridesmaid's dresses and flowers, walking down a long Church aisle to beautiful music, cutting a wedding cake together, and going to some exotic place for a honeymoon, enkindles a strong desire to get married as soon as they can. When a relationship begins to get serious, they push to get married before they are really ready, so that the wedding plans can begin with earnest. The problem is obvious. They may have a great wedding, but a wedding is only a day; a marriage is a lifetime!

"Rebound" relationships can also pose a problem. Some persons, after the breakup of a longstanding relationship, are tempted to rush into a new relationship. They miss the closeness of their past union and want to fill the cavernous gap in their life as soon as possible. They find someone they like, but rather than take the time needed to develop a good relationship, they rush through the "preliminaries" in an effort to get back to where they were previously. They commit to a serious relationship prematurely. Their "rebound" union will work for awhile, but in time overlooked and unresolved difficulties will have to be faced and settled.

The fear of making a commitment

At the other end of the spectrum, there are those persons, who are afraid, even terrified, of making a marital commitment. Whether they were raised in a bad marital situation, had a bad marriage themselves, are fearful of giving up the freedom of their single life, or are simply intimidated by the added responsibilities that marriage entails, they are reluctant to bind themselves in a lifelong marriage.

More often than not, it is the male who tends to be more apprehensive of making a marital commitment. Perhaps, the classic example is the "footloose and fancy free" bachelor who is fearful that becoming involved with a woman will severely cramp his lifestyle. Pursuing a relationship means giving up the pursuit of other women and putting limits on time spent with the guys. It also means the possibility of future support obligations and being "tied down" with a family.

For most of these young males, the fear of making a marital commitment is just a phase. When they meet the "right" young woman, the joy of being with her will be more satisfying than being free and independent. Love will motivate them more than fear.

Peer pressures also come into play here. As a young man gets older and sees his friends getting married and starting families, he begins to rethink his ideas either from a fear of being left out of the mainstream, or as a response to a deep down need for a more fulfilling lifestyle. Many confirmed bachelors, when stirred by either or both of these motivations, suddenly "bite the bullet" and decide for domesticity, often to the surprise of their friends and family.

The fear of making a marital commitment seems especially a problem among recently divorced males. I have had countless women tell me that their formerly divorced male suitors are quite happy to live with them but want no part of marriage. The negative experience of a past relationship plus ongoing financial responsibilities have soured these men on marriage. They want companionship and sex, but not the loss of freedom and the support obligations of marriage.

The deep-seated problems of these commitment fearing men can be overcome but only with a great deal of patience and love. Before they can make a lifelong commitment, they must be convinced that life together with their partner is more valuable than their independence. This realization will take time. There are no shortcuts in making this decision.

Recently, a friend of mine, whose wife had died two years before, became involved with a young woman. The relationship progressed to the point where he wanted her constant companionship but was reluctant to make a marital commitment. He asked her to live with him, and to his great surprise, she said "no." She did not want a partial commitment. If he did not value her enough to make a permanent commitment, she did not want to live with him. They continued seeing each other and their relationship grew stronger. In time, he came to realize that he wanted to share his life with her more than he wanted to keep his independence. His love for her overcame his fears. He proposed marriage and they were married shortly thereafter.

As mentioned before, love is the best reason for making a marital commitment. Ultimately, it alone will overcome the fears of commitment. Even when you have a reluctant partner, getting him or her to commit for any other reason will only set up the conditions for future problems.

There are some persons who have a pathological fear of making a marital commitment. This fear can be manifested by a refusal to continue in a relationship despite a promising beginning, by breaking off a relationship just when it begins to get serious, or by an obsessive desire to live together rather than get married. When fears of this kind are so deep-seated, professional counselling alone can help.

A former student of mine, after having had a bad marriage, decided to live together with her new boyfriend. They cohabited quite happily for thirteen years! As she approached her mid-thirties, she developed a strong desire to have a child. She discussed this matter with him as well as the possibility of getting married, so that the child would be part of a complete family. Surprisingly to her, he bolted the relationship and began living with another woman whom he knew from his office. This second relationship lasted until his new partner also began to talk about marriage, at which point he went back to my former student. They were reconciled until once more she began to talk about marriage. Again, he went back to the other woman. This switching of partners happened several more times. Both women had such low levels of self-esteem that they were willing to accept him back several times despite his callous treatment of them. It was clear that he had an abnormal fear of making a permanent commitment. He eventually left both women and is living together with a third woman. I suspect that he will never make a genuine marital commitment.

Although commitment-phobic persons are few in number, they cause great pain to those who become involved with them. You may think that you can change them but you cannot. Their fear is too deeply rooted. They need help. Unless you are willing to wait while they receive therapy, and it may not work, the best solution is to get out of the relationship as soon as possible.

Readiness to make a marital commitment

At a certain point in a developing relationship, it becomes reasonable for a couple to make a permanent commitment to each other. Defining this point with exactitude is not easy. Most persons just seem to "know" that their union has developed sufficiently to consider marriage. Their "knowledge" is not based simply on some romantic feelings but hopefully is rooted in a careful consideration of many factors, including personal maturity, couple readiness, finances, age, and length of courtship.

1. Personal readiness

As we have said before, it does not make sense to consider getting married if you do not have your own personal life in order. If you do not know what you want out of your own life, how can you realisticallly enter into a union with someone else? How can you plan a life together if you do not even know what you want for yourself?

There are many personal questions that need to be answered before you consider marriage. Do you have "your own act together?" Have you come to grips with who you are and what you want out of life? Do you have some sort of a life plan? Do you respect yourself or do you allow others to trample over your ambitions and accomplishments? Are you able to take responsibility for your affairs or do others dictate how you live? Can you relate with others in a loving way or do you basically use people? Have you done the things you want to do as a single person?

2. Couple readiness

Before a couple get married, as we have seen, it is important that they spend enough time together to explore their mutual compatibility and to determine what they want out of their future relationship. Again, many basic questions need to be answered. How well do you know your partner? How well does he/she know you? Have you seen each other in a wide variety of circumstances? Do you share a wide range of common interests? Is your bond primarily romantic and/or sexual, or do you have a deeper self-giving love for each other? Are your attitudes towards careers, family and religion compatible? Is your relationship egalitarian or does one of you dominate the other? Do you really want to share your future lives together?

3. Financial readiness

Although a couple do not need to be rich to be happy, their relationship will be sorely tested if they do not have adequate finances. How much is enough, as we have seen, will vary from couple to couple. Some partners will not consider marriage without two secure jobs and a mortgage free house. Others are prepared to marry even though they have little or no money at the time of their marriage. What is important is that the couple discuss their monetary situation, agree on what financial level they are prepared to live and then abide by their agreement. A couple can be happy living on a shoestring provided both are willing to live at that level. If they are not willing to sit on milk crates and eat Kraft dinners for a while, then it makes sense for them to wait until they are able to raise sufficient capital to live as they desire.

4. Age

There is no "best" age for someone to get married. In North America, the average age at the time of first marriage is about 23-26 for women and 25-28 for men. This seems to be a reasonable age for most couples to marry, but age by itself should not be the key factor in their decision to marry. Other considerations, like personal maturity and couple readiness, should weigh more heavily. Also, chronological age is not always indicative of the level of maturity a person has attained. A few rare individuals are sufficiently mature to get married at sixteen, others will not be ready until they are thirty and still others will never be ready.

Studies do indicate that the younger a person is at the time of marriage, the more likely the union will break up. This is particularly true if one or both is a teenager when the marriage occurs. The main reason for this phenomenon is that many persons in their teens or early twenties have not sufficiently developed their personalities or their abilities to be able to carry out a marital commitment. They often do not have an adequate grasp of what they want out of life, let alone know what they want out of a marriage. While admitting that there are some exceptions, most experts recommend against youthful marriages.

5. Length of courtship

How long should a couple go together before they are ready to get married? Again, there is no optimal amount of time for every couple. I know some couples who have good marriages after courting each other for only a few months, and others who have bad marriages after going together for ten years. The length of time a pair go out together before marriage is not necessarily a determinant of how good their marriage will be. However, as a general rule, the longer a couple know each other, the better their marital prospects.

What is especially important is not the length of a couple's courtship, but the quality of their time together. Have they spent enough time together to know each other well? Are they sure that they want to marry one another? Do they have a good grasp of what they want out of their marriage? Are they ready and willing to take on the responsibilities of married life? These questions and others need to be answered before they marry. The length of time required to answer them will vary from couple to couple.

From experience, I think that most couples should go out with each other for at least a year before they make a decision to get married. In most cases, it takes at least a year for a couple to determine their basic compatibility, more if the pair are in their teens or early twenties. A period of a year is also advisable so that the partners can see each other during all seasons. How persons live during the summer is not the same as how they live during the winter.

Being faithful to your vows

A marriage does not come ready made. Your initial exchange of vows binds you together but your union is by no means complete. It will take time and creative effort to fulfill the promise of your relationship.

Like all commitments, a marriage commitment concerns the future. It is a deliberate attempt to reach beyond the present and bind your lives together in the days to come. If your marriage is to be realized, both of you must continually reaffirm that initial commitment.

Throughout your relationship, you must decide whether your original promises are worth renewing. If your marriage is a good one, this will be no problem. The warmth and love that are present will move you to reaffirm your marriage with little thought to the contrary. However, if your union is bad, at every troubled juncture, you will have to decide whether you really want to remain married. As was said before, a marriage does not come ready made. It is willfully chosen throughout your life together.

Even in the best of marriages, reaffirming your original commitment will sometimes be difficult. The positive feelings that drew you together at the beginning of your relationship will not always be present. At times, you will have to reaffirm your union when you do not especially feel good about your partner. In spite of these negative feelings, you must "grit your teeth" and do those things that will renew the relationship. Otherwise, the marriage will not survive.

Sooner or later every couple will have an argument that will make one or both angry. Suddenly, the good feelings about each other are gone. There is hurt and a desire to lash out at each other. If the relationship is to survive, the couple must try to work out an acceptable solution to their impasse in the midst of their anger and hurt. They will have to swallow their pride, restrain their impulses to say and do negative things, be ready to apologize for any deliberate hurtful words or actions, and get back to the business of finding a satisfactory resolution to their problem. This will not always be easy to do, but it must be done if the relationship is to continue. The partners must override their negative feelings if their union is to be maintained.

Sometimes, it is not negative feelings that have to be fought but positive feelings. A classic example is that of a married man who meets a pretty woman while on a business trip. She is obviously attracted to him. He, in turn, quite taken by her sexiness and charm, makes initial efforts to know her better. In time, he is tempted to pursue the relationship in a more serious way, knowing full well that if he does, it could lead to greater involvement. Lest he jeopardize the good union with his wife, he must put a damper on the new relationship now before he becomes too involved. This will not be easy under the circumstances but if he truly values his marriage, he must do it. His original commitment to his wife must be reaffirmed in the face of his new found attraction to this woman.

When you get married, you promise each other that you will make every effort to foster the love bond that exists between the two of you. You do this without knowing what the future will bring. Feelings and circumstances will arise that will undoubtedly strain your original commitment. Only if you are willing to reaffirm your original commitment in the face of these contrary feelings and circumstances can you ever hope to realize the promise of your relationship. Your marriage will not just happen. It comes into being only through your continued fidelity to your original vows.

In my experience, the couples who have the best marriages are those that have a very strong commitment to stay together. When problems arise, they are not willing to give up on their marriages. They will make every effort to resolve their difficulties. Even though anger, resentment and conflict may be present, they remain confident that these problems can be overcome. They are willing to weather the storms because they truly believe that blue skies will come again.

Summary

A commitment is statement of serious intent made by one person to another to do or forswear something. When two persons marry, they make a lifelong commitment to share the whole of their lives. Their commitment to marry should flow out of their mutual love. If the partners do not love each other or their love is weak, their commitment will quickly become a ball and chain rather than a perfecting of their life together.

Marriage is a most serious commitment. It should not be entered into lightly. If a couple marry before they are ready, they risk creating a bond that may not endure. On the other hand, if they have a strong love for each other and have adequately explored their relationship, they should not be afraid to get married. They should not let unfounded fears deter them.

A good marriage comes into being over time. The exchange of the vows is just the beginning. Every day the couple must reaffirm their initial commitment. Sometimes, this will be difficult, and yet, it is the couple's faithfulness to their initial vows that enables them to build their own unique marriage. The greater their loyalty to each other, the greater the chance that their relationship will continue and flourish. A good marriage does not come ready made; it is created through the love and sweat of the two partners.

DISCUSSION QUESTIONS

1. Do you understand marriage to be a commitment that lasts until the death of one of the partners?
2. Are you ready to make a permanent commitment to your partner?
3. Are you afraid of making a lifelong commitment? Why?
4. Are you old enough to get married?
5. Have you been going together long enough to be ready to make a lifelong commitment?

CHAPTER TWELVE

EQUALITY

The issue of equality is front and center in men-women relationships nowadays. Feminists have been fighting hard to undo the long tradition of male domination within our Western culture. In recent years, their efforts have been responsible for more equal participation of men and women in the home and the workplace. Within the home, there has been a more equal sharing of roles. An increasing number of husbands and wives share the housekeeping and child rearing tasks. "Breadwinning" is no longer seen as primarily and simply the husband's duty. The work place is filled with more women pursuing financial and personal rewards. Better opportunities exist in business, politics, the professions, and several other fields previously closed to women. The number of female executives is also on the rise.

However, as feminists are quick to point out, women may have come a long way, but they have a long way to go. Despite recent egalitarian advances in the home, husbands still do not pick up their fair share of work around the house. When children arrive, most often it is the wives who sacrifice their full time jobs to stay home for a few years with the young ones. If the marriage breaks down, women are more frequently left in a severe financial bind. Most single mothers live below the poverty line. Although almost as many women as men are in the work force, women earn only about two thirds as much as men in comparable jobs. There are disproportionately fewer women in corporate boardrooms, executive positions, higher paid professions, and elected political offices.

Although we are moving toward a more egalitarian society, we are clearly still in a transitional phase. Many women and men support the liberation of women from fixed roles and expectations, but opposing forces still exist. Some traditionalists are still wedded to old ways and do not want a change. Certain ethnic and religious groups have long patriarchal traditions that die hard. Many men see the new woman as a threat to their identity and jobs. Sociobiologists argue that men and women are inherently different and best suited for the roles they have traditionally played.

No evidence for male supremacy

Although there are obvious differences between the sexes, to my mind, there is no justification for supporting male supremacy. In past societies, when physical strength was more important for survival, male brawn gave men a clear advantage in running the society and the home. In our present North American society, technological advances have made physical strength much less significant. Intellectual and emotional talents are more highly prized. Despite age old prejudices, there is no conclusive evidence that women are any less intelligent or emotionally sound than men. In fact, as women have become better educated and been given better opportunities, it has become clear that their intellectual and emotional attributes make them just as capable as men in the workplace.

In the past, frequent pregnancies also kept women in a subservient position. Nowadays North American women get pregnant less often. The physical encumbrances that exist while they carry and breast-feed their babies take up only a small proportion of most women's adult lives and can no longer be used as a justification for keeping them in an overall subordinate position within the society.

The longstanding argument that women have a "maternal instinct," making them more adept at caring for children and less suited for work outside of the home, has not been supported by empirical studies. Most social scientists today hold that the socialization of women from their earliest years accounts for their greater willingness and ability to care for children. Recently, as more men have taken on childrearing roles, it has become clear that both men and women can raise children caringly and effectively. A woman's biology may determine her childbearing role but it does not necessarily tie her to a childrearing role.

An unsettling transition period

The movement toward a more egalitarian society is much needed and long overdue. However, the transition is unsettling for many individuals and is causing much confusion. For example, some men who were raised in traditional homes are having difficulties adjusting to a new egalitarian mentality. In the past, they were waited on hand and foot by their mothers and sisters while at home. Now, they are being asked to share the household work by their liberated girlfriends. Their old habits die hard.

What it means to be feminine or masculine nowadays is not always clear for many individuals. Is it more feminine for a woman to want to stay at home when her children are young or to work full time? Can a woman be assertive without being considered a "bitch?" If a man is tender and compassionate, is he more fully masculine or is he a "wimp?" Can he be a "real" man if he stays home for a few years to care for the children?

Relations between women and men have also become unsure. Can a woman initiate dates and sexual advances, or will she be considered "forward" by doing so? Should a man open doors and pull out chairs for a woman, or will he be called a "chauvinist pig?" When a couple go out together, who pays? Is he expected to pay, does she pay, or do they both pay?

Given the uncertain climate, it is especially important nowadays for a couple to discuss their sexual role expectations. Do they believe in sexual equality, and if so, how do they intend to bring it about in their union?

Equality: its meaning within a relationship

Equality in a relationship basically means that both partners are treated as equals. One is not seen as superior or more important than the other. Specifically, equal treatment means:

1) granting one another equal respect;
2) giving equally to the relationship;
3) sharing the workload of the partnership in an equal manner.

1) Equal respect

Granting one another equal respect is an imperative for an equal relationship. It means that both partners see each other as having equal worth. The needs, goals and aspirations of both are comparably valued and equal efforts are made by both parties to realize them within the relationship. The wants and desires of one partner do not take precedence over those of the other because of some preconceived superiority.

When the partners do not have equal respect for one another, the inevitable result will be an unbalanced relationship where one person gets more out of the union than the other. If a young man was raised in a traditional ethnic home and believes that men are superior to women, he will expect that his needs and goals should take precedence over hers. She will be expected to cater to his desires. Seeing himself as the superior partner, he will try to control her life and tell her how to live. If she accepts these traditional beliefs, she consigns herself to a lesser status in the relationship. If she does not, she will have serious difficulties trying to protect her personal integrity and effecting changes in his attitudes and those of his family.

To say that two partners should respect each other as equals does not mean that their abilities, prior accomplishments or social status are equal. It is most unlikely that they will be. Invariably, one partner will have greater intellectual or physical gifts, earn more money, have better child rearing skills, or have greater social status. Although these individual talents and achievements are noteworthy, they must *not* be seen as reasons for viewing one person in the relationship as being superior to the other, thereby warranting favored treatment in the relationship.

The growth and development of both partners, not just one, is the goal of a *full* marital partnership. Just because a person earns more money, is a public figure, has greater intelligence, or has a higher status in the community does not entitle him or her to preferential treatment in the relationship. A good marriage should not benefit one person at the expense of the other. It is created to benefit *both* partners equally.

To illustrate, let us take the case of a young woman who has a successful modelling career. She earns three times as much money as her partner and has greater public recognition and acclaim. If her achievements and status by themselves *entitle* her to having a primary place in the relationship, then his needs and goals will have to be subordinate. He will be a second class citizen in his own marriage. For a time, he may be willing to bask in her glory, but sooner or later, if he has any personal pride, he will become unhappy playing second fiddle. He will want a shared relationship where his personal growth is as important as hers.

In an equal relationship, a couple may mutually agree to give precedence to the talents of one partner at a particular time, but it must be a *mutual* decision. It should not automatically be assumed that the person with the superior earning power or status should take preference. Returning to the above example, the couple may mutually decide that promoting her modelling career at this time, while she is in demand, is most advantageous for the two of them. In practice, this would mean that if her work requires a move, he would be willing to follow her, but not vice versa. Even though he desires children, they would postpone them until later so as not to interrupt her career. Their decision is based on what both see as mutually advantageous, not on some predetermined superiority on her part.

At some time in the future, the couple may reach a shared decision that it is better for their relationship if her career no longer takes precedence. She may be tired of working full time or being constantly in the public eye. They may find that her career limits their time together and agree that she should cut back for the sake of the relationship. His career may be taking off and both may believe that it is time to concentrate on his needs. Whatever the reason, the decision to change will respect both person's interests.

2) Equal giving

In a good relationship, both partners must work equally hard in promoting the union. One person cannot give significantly less than the other.

It is frustrating to be in a relationship where you feel that you are giving significantly more than your partner. To illustrate, you give up a night with your friends so that you can spend more time with your partner, but he or she does not reciprocate. You control spending your money to help build a better nest egg for your marriage, but your partner continues to spend money like water. You are willing to spend time with your partner's friends, but he or she is not willing to make the effort to come to know your friends. You make efforts to work out common difficulties, but your mate does not really care. After awhile, you feel cheated. You are making real efforts to promote the relationship, but your partner is not. In a full relationship, both partners must give equally to the union.

Equal giving does not mean that every good act by one partner must be reciprocated by the other. To say the least, that would become tedious. What is needed is parity of giving over the course of the relationship. At one time, one person may give more than the other, but at other times, the other will be more giving. In the end, their efforts will more or less balance.

Sometimes conditions arise that do not allow both partners always to contribute equally to the relationship. If your boyfriend has a heavy work schedule in the fall or is writing exams and essays at University, he will not be able to give as much time to the relationship as you can. In your kindness, you may go out of your way to help him by washing his dishes, buying his groceries and making coffee for him while he works or writes essays, knowing that he cannot reciprocate. You are also aware that success in his work or studies is important for both of you in the long run. Hopefully, at some time in the future, when you have similar needs, he will reciprocate in kind.

3) Sharing the workload equally

Running a household requires that certain jobs be done. Food must be prepared, dishes washed, rugs vacuumed, and the bathroom cleaned. As well, the car needs to be serviced, the lawns mowed and leaves raked. When children come along, they must be fed, clothed, babysat, and taken to scouts or soccer games. The list is endless. As well, one or both partners will need a paying job to provide financial support for the whole enterprise.

When a couple share a household, it is only fair that they apportion the workload as equally as possible. Both should pick up their fair share of the work. Neither partner should expect the other to pick up a heavier load on an ongoing basis. On a temporary basis, as illustrated by the example above, it may be necessary for one partner to pick up a greater portion of the load than the other. However, in the long run, the work should be divided as equally as possible.

Creating egalitarian sexual roles

In the past, when male and female marital roles were more clearly defined, a couple knew what to expect before they married. Nowadays, under the influence of the women's movement and the tight economy, roles have become more flexible and it is no longer clear in advance how a couple will divide their workload. Each couple must decide for themselves how they want to share their responsibilities. Let us look at four common approaches with an eye to determining how equality can be realized in each of them.

a. The traditional model

Some couples, a minority, still choose to marry along traditional lines. The husband is the main breadwinner and does the traditional male chores around the house, like mowing the lawn, doing household repairs and caring for the car. The wife may work outside the home prior to the arrival of the children, but once the children arrive, she stays at home until the last child is in high school or perhaps has left home. She is responsible for the care of the household, the cooking, the laundry, and the bulk of the care for the children.

Although this arrangement sounds like a male dominant household, it does not have to be. If the wishes of both partners are respected in choosing the model, the workload is equally divided and both are happy in it, it can hardly be viewed as male domination. It would be if she was forced to take on a submissive role in the union.

Two friends of mine chose a traditional but egalitarian arrangement. They both wanted a large family and believed that it was best for the children if a parent was home full time with them. Since he was a gifted academic whose writings were influential in his field, both agreed, even though she had solid academic credentials as well, that his career should take precedence. She was willing to be the primary person responsible for child care and the upkeep of the household. Despite the appearance of a patriarchal union, the desires of both persons were respected in working out the union. They saw each other as equals and were happy in their marriage.

There can be problems with pursuing the traditional arrangement. Some women flourish in the home setting; others quickly become bored and look for outside stimulation. They enjoy their children but find spending most of their day at home unexciting and tedious. They want something else to do. When these feelings of boredom arise, they must be acknowledged and discussed openly. It will probably be necessary for the couple to modify their relationship.

Although the wife's work should be valued as highly as her husband's, it is a fact that in North America working outside the home is generally more esteemed than staying at home and caring for the children. This attitude sometimes creeps into a traditional couple's relationship, despite their original egalitarian intent. The result is that his work becomes more important than hers, and the relationship becomes progressively more one-sided.

It is disturbing that so many people in our society consider raising children to be a secondary task. We all know how badly children suffer when their parents do not adequately care for them. We also know how advantageous it is for children to come from a loving home. When a couple decide to have children, their care must be a top priority. Therefore, if the wife stays home to look after the children, her role cannot be seen as secondary. Raising healthy, well adjusted children is no less important than breadwinning.

Although the actual care of children in a traditional union falls primarily on the mother, this does not mean that the father should have no part in the process. Some men believe that if they do the breadwinning, that is all that should be asked of them. They spend little time with their children and give little help to their wives in raising them. This approach is fair neither to the children nor the wife. When a couple decide to have children, both are responsible for raising them. Although the wife may be the primary care giver in this arrangement, the husband is also a parent and must make time to be with the children. If he neglects them, they will invariably feel rejected and will be hurt by his lack of concern. As well, his wife will come to resent his lack of help in caring for them. Child care, especially during the early years, is more than a nine to five occupation, and it is unfair for the wife to have to do it all. The husband should pick up his fair share.

b. The semi-traditional model

Some couples have no problems with both partners working full time outside of the home prior to the arrival of children. However, they feel strongly that infants and toddlers need parental care rather than surrogate care during their formative years. Therefore, they believe that one or other should stay home when their children are very young. Usually it is the woman, but in a small number of cases it is the man. After the last child reaches school age, the parenting partner usually returns to full time work.

This approach can be egalitarian providing the wishes of both partners are respected in the arrangement, and there is an equal sharing of their workload during the various phases of the relationship.

A major problem arises here for the woman, who by staying at home during her children's formative years, must forego advancement in her field and may even risk the possibility of not being able to return to her original position or even losing her career. Some women are quite willing to take this risk but others find it to be a wrench. It is difficult to spend several years establishing a career, only to have to give it up or to forego opportunities for advancement. The decision to stay at home temporarily involves a real concession. Hopefully, when the time comes, her appreciative husband will help to facilitate her re-entry into the work force; and, should the occasion arise, he will be willing to make a similar sacrifice.

Some women try to cushion this decision by choosing employment where it is possible to take off a few years without penalty, or to work part time for awhile. This is a good strategy, provided the woman does not have to forego a field of work that she strongly prefers or is specially trained to do.

c. The househusband alternative

In a small but increasing number of cases, the husband stays at home to look after the children, either on a short or long term basis, while his wife works full time. These arrangements are similar to the prior two, except that the roles are reversed.

In my experience, I have found that men who have chosen to be househusbands have generally enjoyed their experience and have especially appreciated the opportunity to spend time with their children. However, only a few of them expressed any willingness to do it for a long period of time. Among my male students, a similar outlook exists. Many are willing to stay at home for a time, but only a handful expressed any interest in doing it on a long term basis. These feelings exist in part because most men see the pursuit of a career as being an important part of their life cycle, and there still exists a definite societal stigma against being a long term "Mr. Mom." It may be acceptable, even admirable, for a "liberated man" to stay home for a few years, but eyebrows begin to get raised when a man chooses to be a long term househusband. Whether that perception will change in the future remains to be seen.

In the long run, if women are to achieve greater equality in the workplace, it is important that more men be willing to stay at home with the children while their spouse is working. As long as more women than men choose to remain at home, men will continue to have greater opportunities in the world of work outside the home. By opting out of the workplace when their children are young, women leave during their prime years for advancement, thereby giving their male peers a decided advantage. This advantage will remain until as many men as women decide to stay at home to care for children on a part time or long term basis.

d. The dual income model

During the past twenty-five years, the number of married women employed full time has increased sharply. Almost as many wives are in the workplace as husbands. Over fifty per cent of them have children under three. The dual income[1] family has become commonplace in our time and will probably be the option chosen by most young couples.

There are several reasons why both partners choose to work full time, even when the children are young. Some simply want the personal fulfillment that comes from working outside the home. Others basically want to improve their standard of living. The extra income allows them to have luxuries they otherwise could not afford. But most partners both work just to make ends meet. In an economy where one breadwinner often does not earn enough to keep the family above the poverty line, a second income is a necessity.

Before children are present, there are usually not too many problems in sharing the workload in a dual income household. It is mainly a matter of dividing the basic tasks around the apartment or house, like cooking, laundry and cleaning. However, when children arrive, the workload is increased enormously and the potential for serious problems is present.

The work involved in caring for babies and toddlers is usually poorly understood by young people who have not grown up around young children. Experts estimate that young children require at least thirteen hours of care a day. Unlike pets or toys, small children cannot be put away after you are done playing with them. They demand and need constant attention during their waking hours. They must be fed, changed, clothed, and bathed. They want to play, be told stories, run around the house or yard, get into things that they should not, and be cuddled. They cry, get cranky and have temper tantrums. If siblings are present, there will be arguments and fights. Even when they go to bed, they do not always sleep through the night. The process of looking after their needs, educating them and loving them is continuous and time consuming. Most parents consider their children to be blessings, but they are also a lot of work, especially when they are young.

If you have never been around small children, I highly recommend that you spend some time with friends or relatives who have some. Talk with them about the care needed, how tired they get and the sense of confinement that often comes with children. Offer to babysit the children for a day or two to get a feel for the kind of time demands that are present. Your friends or relatives will probably jump at the chance to give you the opportunity!

When children are present in a dual income family, it makes eminent sense that the additional workload be divided evenly. Unfortunately, recent studies show that many husbands in dual income households do not pick up their fair share. Their traditional upbringing or just plain lethargy are the main reasons for their minimal help. This is a potential problem that a couple should begin discussing *before* they marry. Although they may not be able to discuss all of the specifics, they can at least agree on the principle of sharing the workload and on some general ways in which this can be accomplished. After a child is born, they can sit down and work out particulars of sharing their new workload. If the husband fails to pick up his fair share of the chores, the wife should firmly remind him of their agreement. "You said that you would...." If he remains recalcitrant, further discussion will be required and perhaps a more radical solution, like hiring a maid service to do the household cleaning, may be needed.

Some women, either because they are afraid to confront their husbands, or because they honestly believe or have been conditioned to believe that they can do it all, fall into the "superwoman syndrome." They work full time outside of the home and then pick up the traditional woman's role at home. This is equivalent to doing two full time jobs and will inevitably lead to fatigue, depression and resentment. If a couple make a decision to both work outside the home, they must also make a decision to share the domestic chores.

Even when the workload is divided equally, a dual income marriage with young children, is not easy. The couple's overall workload is much greater than in a traditional arrangement. In a dual income union, two full time jobs outside the home as well as the domestic duties must be divided, as opposed to just one outside job and the domestic duties. A dual working couple's day will be quite full. Prior to going to work in the morning, they must get the children ready for the sitter or the day care center. After work, the children must be picked up, supper prepared and some "quality" time spent with them. Afterwards, other chores like laundry and shopping will have to be done. On the weekends, extra time is usually spent with the children because the couple have been away during the week. Other household chores, not completed during the week, will also have to be done.

Most dual income couples find that their exhausting schedules limit the time they are able to spend with friends and family, or doing outside activities. Many also complain that their sex lives are diminished because they are often too tired during the week to have sexual relations.

A key to a successful dual income marriage is good organization. With so much to do and so little time to do it, it is critical for a couple to arrange their time carefully. Another key is the willingness to sacrifice non-essentials. Many do not clean their house as often and learn to ignore the dishes piled in the sink. They engage in fewer outside activities and socialize with a smaller circle of friends.

The majority of dual income couples, in my experience, are happy with their lifestyles. They enjoy their careers or jobs and do not want to give them up. They also enjoy their family life. Despite the hectic pace of their lives, they would not have it any other way. However, some dual income couples find the workload too heavy and feel overwhelmed by the demands of their lifestyle. Eventually, where possible, they reduce their outside working hours. Usually the wife will either quit her job or work part time.

Child care

As mentioned earlier, child care must be a priority in a marriage. It makes no sense to have children if they are not going to be looked after properly. When a couple with young children both work full time, they must make every effort to insure that the care of their children while they are absent is good, fulfilling and even exceeds their personal standards and expectations. If they cannot find such care, they should reconsider their full time work arrangements.

Sometimes a couple will be fortunate enough to have a trustworthy parent, relative or neighbor who is willing to look after the children. More often, they will have to resort to nannies, sitters or day care centers. In selecting a nanny or full time sitter, the couple should get references and be assured that the person chosen will be caring and responsive to their children. They should know what kind of daily routine the children will have and how they will be disciplined. They should also know if the sitter will be looking after other children, and how that will affect the care of their own children.

If a day care is considered, the pair should inspect the facilities, visit during care hours, unannounced if possible, and consult other couples who have used the center. They should also become familiar with the qualifications of the employees, the ratio of children to caregivers, the children's daily routine, the kinds of food they will eat, and the nature of the educational program. Above all, they should feel confident that the caregivers will be warm and responsive to their children.

Cost and availability are other factors that must be weighed by a couple in choosing a sitter or day care. The cost of good child care presently ranges from $20 to $50 per day. This can be prohibitive for some couples, especially if they are at the lower end of the income scale or have two or more children. They may be able to find a spot in a day care subsidized by the government. Even when the cost is within reason, good sitters or day cares may not always be available or easily accessible. Most cities have a shortage of day care facilities and sitters. It is not uncommon for parents to enrol their children at a day care center even before they are born. Some smaller towns and communities simply do not have any facilities at all. Being employed at times other than the traditional nine to five, like working evenings in a restaurant, may make finding a sitter or day care especially difficult.

If reasonably priced accessible child care is not available, the temptation is to risk less satisfactory arrangements. To my way of thinking, that is a mistake. If a couple really love their children, it is better for them to lower their standard of living for awhile rather than jeopardize their children's upbringing.

Experts disagree about whether it is harmful for young children to spend so much time with a sitter or in a day care center. Some hold that if children, three years old or younger, spend too much time with surrogate caregivers, they will not bond properly with their own parents. Others argue that these studies are inconclusive. In recent years, child psychologists have specifically criticized putting infants (under one year) in day care centers. They argue there is mounting evidence that the hours of non-maternal care leads to more insecure relations with the mother, increased risks of emotional and behavioral problems in later childhood, and the higher possibility of aggressive and disobedient behavior. Other experts dispute these claims, again saying that the evidence is inconclusive.

In deciding whether to have your children looked after by full time sitters or day care centers, especially young infants, it is advisable to consult friends and family for advice and to read all the available literature. However, you should always remember that what works for someone else's child may not work for yours. Every child is unique and will respond in different ways to surrogate care. Some children seem to thrive; others are troubled. Continual watchfulness and flexibility are necessary.

Some concluding remarks

Most young couples nowadays want an egalitarian relationship. It provides the best environment for them to grow and develop within a marriage. However, its realization is not always easy. The process of working out a relationship of equals is best begun long before the marriage. If you feel that your partner does not equally respect your needs and goals, discuss the matter. If you do not think that your partner is giving to the relationship as fully as you are, talk to him or her about it. If the two of you both intend to pursue careers, it is important to begin discussing now how you will share the workload around the house, especially when children arrive. An equal relationship does not just happen; the couple must work at it, and the sooner they get at it, the better.

The issue of sexual equality within a relationship cannot be entirely separated from the larger issue of sexual equality within the whole of our society. Although a couple may deal with each other as equals, they exist in a societal environment that neither fully accepts women as equals nor makes adequate provisions for the new work situations of egalitarian couples. Sooner or later these realities will impinge on their relationship. The unequal earning ability of men and women with comparable qualifications will often dictate whose job will take precedence in a marriage. The lack of adequate day care facilities, and the inflexible work hours and parental policies of most businesses make pursuing a dual income marriage difficult for many couples. In working out an egalitarian relationship, a couple must take these societal inequities into account. In the long run, if they are truly concerned about sexual equality within their relationship, it is incumbent upon them to work for greater sexual equality within the larger society.

DISCUSSION QUESTIONS

1. Do you believe that a wife should be submissive to her husband?
2. Do you and your partner respect each other's needs and aspirations equally?
3. Does your partner give as much to your relationship as you do?
4. Do you believe that the husband should be the primary breadwinner in the family?
5. Do you and your partner want a dual income marriage? How do you propose to take care of the children?
6. Do you believe in putting young children in day care centers?
7. As a man, would you consider being a househusband?

CHAPTER THIRTEEN

SEX

North American sexual attitudes and behavior have changed dramatically in recent years. Prior to the sixties, the prevailing attitude was that sexual intercourse should be restricted to marriage and, for the most part, unmarried couples did limit their sexual expression to non-coital activities. All of this changed with the advent of the birth control pill and other effective contraceptive measures. These new methods of birth control enabled unmarried couples, without fear of pregnancy, to engage in sexual relations more frequently. They were spurred on by a spate of films, books and magazines of the period that encouraged greater premarital sexual openness and activity. The result was a rapid change in sexual behavior and attitudes. The early Kinsey studies of sexual behavior among pre-1960 unmarrieds showed that approximately 25% of the women and 50% of the men engaged in premarital relations. Recent studies indicate that as many as 75% of both unmarried men and women have had sexual intercourse by the time they are twenty-five. Furthermore, these recent studies show that over 80% of the adult population, married and unmarried, endorse premarital sexual relations, at least in some cases.

When I talk to my students and other young people nowadays, there is no question that there has been a significant change in sexual attitudes and behavior since my generation. Many young men and women openly discuss their sexual experiences with me. Many have had sex with several partners, engaged in oral sex, tried various sexual positions, and in some cases have experimented with kinkier forms of sex. What has become clear is that for many young men and women, sexual intercourse has become a *normal expectation* during an ongoing relationship. Unlike my generation, it is not something reserved for marriage.

Not all young people subscribe to these sexual values. There are still a vocal number, usually coming from traditional backgrounds, that advocate waiting until marriage before having sexual intercourse. However, they are clearly in the minority. The great majority endorse premarital sexual relations, especially if the couple are "in love."

Sex as normal and natural

It is natural for a couple to be sexually attracted and to want to hold and caress each other. Sex can be a tender and exciting sensual experience. It can bind a couple together and can be an emotional and physical high in their relationship. Nevertheless, despite the joys of sex, sometimes sexual relating can have adverse consequences on a couple's overall union. Overindulging in sex too early in a relationship can mislead a couple into believing that they have a deep love relation when all they really have is a strong sexual attraction. Unprotected intercourse can lead to unwanted pregnancies or sexually transmitted diseases. Some callous individuals, under the guise of love, still seduce unwitting or unwilling partners into having sex. In their unbridled quest for sexual gratification, they may even use psychological or physical force.

Despite the greater sexual openness and freedom of the present age, regrettably the evils of irresponsible sex remain. In fact, they have actually increased in the past generation. The incidence of unwed pregnancies, sexually transmitted diseases, date rape, and sexual abuse are higher than at any other time in this century. The solution to these problems is clearly not to return to the puritanical attitudes of the past. It is a mistake to regard sex as inherently evil and to repress all sexual thoughts and desires. A better approach is to see our sexual relating as basically good but capable of being misused. Just as our desire to eat is good because it enables us to nourish ourselves, but can be abused through overeating or self-induced starvation, so too our desire to relate sexually is good because it enables us to express our love for our partner and to reproduce the species, but is able to be misused through irresponsible and overindulgent behavior. What is needed, then, to overcome these sexual evils is not repression but a more reasonable and responsible approach to our sexual activity.

Sex is a human activity

There are some prominent thinkers today who would argue that taking a reasonable and responsible approach to our sexual desires is inherently impossible. Whether we want to admit it or not, our sexual passions are basically uncontrollable animalistic cravings. They just happen to us and we really cannot do anything about them. As such, our sexual acts can neither be responsible or irresponsible. To say that a particular sexual act is irresponsible, is simply to voice a feeling of disapproval conditioned in us by our society.

I disagree. I grant that our sexual feelings, like other feelings, often just happen to us. We get sexually aroused sometimes without really intending to do it. I also agree that when our sexual feelings are strong, it is extremely difficult not to indulge them. Initial sexual feelings are not so hard to control, but when they are fanned by sensual stimuli, continual fantasizing and/or physical caressing, they can become so intense that it is almost impossible not to give in to them. Nevertheless, we can make conscious decisions about how to respond to our erotic urgings. Although many of our physiological sexual responses are outside of our control, like increased heart rate, heavier breathing and changes in our sexual organs, we can determine whether we will touch, hold and caress one another. We can decide whether to have intercourse or not. We can choose whether to make our relating a manifestation of love or a way of manipulating the other for some personal gain.

Within any ongoing sexual union, there will be times when it will be necessary to control sexual desires. Differing desires, sickness, fatigue, and the unexpected presence of children will all create situations where sexual desires cannot be satisfied and must be controlled. Sexual control is part and parcel of any intimate man-woman relationship.

Sex, then, is a human activity, not just an animal activity. Our sexual desires are not uncontrollable feelings that totally cloud our reason. They may be extremely strong at times but they do not have to be acted upon any more than we have to act upon strong feelings of anger or jealousy. We can *choose* to give these feelings full rein or to be restrained in responding to them. It may be difficult at times not to act on them, but it is clearly possible. We do not have to be slaves to our sexual passions.

Humanizing sexual relations

As actions able to be controlled by intelligence and will, our sexual relations should be guided by the larger norms that govern all interpersonal relations. That is to say, they should be caring, knowledgeable, respectful, free from coercion, and responsible. In a close relationship, they should especially be loving.

Some couples tend to separate their sexual behavior from the rest of their relationship. They say that they love each other, but when it comes to sex they engage in actions that can be quite hurtful to one another and their relationship. For example, some couples have unprotected sexual intercourse without giving any real thought to the possible consequences for their union. They seem oblivious to the fact that they are risking a pregnancy that could be awkward and embarrassing for the woman and could put severe strains on their relationship. Although they say they love each other and see their sexual relating as an expression of their love, one wonders why they are willing to risk hurting each other or the continuation of their relationship? Are their sexual relations really an expression of love?

Sexual acts must take into account the well-being of the other if they are to be considered acts of self-giving love. In themselves, sexual relations are not inherently loving. They become loving through the loving intent of the couple. When sexual relations are deliberately coercive or irresponsible, they can hardly be said to be loving!

Being knowledgeable about sex

The sexual expression of love presupposes that the partners understand themselves as sexual beings. If we are going to relate sexually with others, we should know how we function sexually and what are the consequences of our sexual acts. Given that our sexual activity can sometimes be harmful and destructive, it is also important to do some serious thinking about sexual values.

For too long, sex has been viewed as dirty and kept "in the closet." One of the major benefits of the recent sexual revolution has been to bring sex more into the open, enabling us to come to a better understanding of our sexual nature. Unfortunately, there are still many persons who come from backgrounds where sex is viewed negatively and is still not discussed. Studies show that the majority of young persons still get no more than a poor sex education from their parents, and some do not even get that! Informal surveys of my own students support these findings. The fact that sex was never mentioned at home or was talked about only in hushed tones gave them the impression that there was something forbidden about it. Aside from remarks like "Be Careful!" or "Watch out!," they received little guidance regarding their sexual activity. As a result, most of them had to receive their sexual knowledge and values from peers and the media, and perhaps a high school sex education class. Sometimes, they wound up with a fairly balanced view of sexual activity; in many instances, they did not. Regrettably, a few of them came from a background so repressive that they still are extremely uncomfortable with their sexuality and are incapable of normal sexual response.

If you come from a background where sex was never explained or discussed, it is important, if you have not already done so, to find a means of gaining an *adequate* and *correct* knowledge of sexual matters. There are many sources of information. Make an appointment to discuss these matters with your family doctor or visit a local health clinic. Most colleges and universities offer a course on sexuality nowadays that may be worthwhile to take or at least audit. A trip to your local library may help. Don't be shy. Ask the librarian for assistance. There are many good books and videos on the market today. If you are a religious person, and know a priest or minister in whom you have confidence, you might talk to him or her. Friends can be helpful, but some of them are misinformed, so be selective. Films, television and magazines present a wide range of materials, but oftentimes the knowledge presented is incomplete and the values confusing. What is important in this quest is that you come to appreciate and accept your own sexuality, and develop a good set of guidelines for your sexual conduct.

Communicating about sex

When you are in a relationship, it is important to talk with your partner about sexual matters, especially about your sexual expectations and values. What kind of sexual expression do you feel is right between the two of you? What type of sexual caressing do you enjoy? Is premarital sex appropriate in your relationship? Are you knowledgeable about birth control? How do you feel about using particular contraceptive methods? In an era of AIDS, it is quite legitimate, if not vital, to discuss your past sexual histories, at least in their broad outlines. Discussing past relationships may not be easy, but it is important to know whether having sexual relations will put you at risk of getting a sexually transmitted disease. In some situations, it may even be necessary to consider the feasibility of testing for sexual diseases.

Throughout the relationship, it is important to communicate about your sexual activity. If you or your partner do not understand how the other feels about certain sexual advances or activities, it makes sense to ask. Don't guess! Sometimes body language can indicate your partner's thoughts and feelings, but not always. When in doubt, talk about it. This may be difficult but it is important to make the effort. Sex is a significant part of your relationship and needs to be openly discussed.

Not only should the troublesome aspects of your sexual relationship be disclosed, so too should the good parts. It always helps to make positive remarks about your partner's sexual activity where pertinent. "I like the way you kiss me!" "You look sexy in that outfit!" "I enjoyed our time together last night!"

Respecting sexual wishes

Although your partner may want to relate sexually with you, ultimately you have the final say whether or not and to what extent you will respond. Your wishes in the matter are paramount. After all, it is your body, and more importantly, it is your conscience. You have to live with the guilt or the feelings of uneasiness that will result if you engage in unwanted sexual relations. In the end, you must respect your own feelings and moral values.

Just as you want your partner to respect your sexual wishes, so too you must be willing to respect your partner's wishes for refusing to relate sexually. Your partner may have well founded reasons for wanting to refrain from sex. He or she may be morally or religiously opposed to heavy sexual involvement before marriage, or may simply believe that it is not right at this stage in your relationship. In some cases, no reason at all may be articulated, just a feeling that it isn't right or desirable at this time. Whatever the reason, or lack thereof, your partner's wishes must be respected. Sexual relating should be mutually chosen. One person should not impose his or her will upon the other.

Continual reluctance to relate sexually, particularly to have sexual intercourse, may cause you or your partner to be quite frustrated. Discussion over time may help the two of you to understand and accept your divergent viewpoints. However, if no reconciliation is possible, you will ultimately have to decide whether to continue as a couple or to leave. If you are the reluctant one, you will have to trust that your partner values you enough that he or she will be willing to forego the satisfaction of certain sexual pleasures at this time. However, if he or she really wants a more sexually responsive person, then perhaps it is best to part company. It makes no sense to engage in sexual acts that you are uneasy doing just to keep a partner. You will ultimately be troubled, and unsettled ground does not provide a strong foundation for a relationship.

Respecting your partner also means that you do not exploit him or her in your sexual relations. It is essentially dishonest to tell your partner how much you love him or her when all you really want is to relieve your sexual tensions or put another "notch on the bedpost." It is also dishonest, and ultimately foolish, to use sex primarily as an instrument to entice your partner into staying with you or marrying you. If your partner stays with you primarily because you satisfy his or her sexual appetite, you have a poor basis for marriage. Sex is not a substitute for love!

Giving free consent to sexual relations

Perhaps one of the most disturbing aspects of contemporary sexual activity among young persons is the high incidence of date rape and date sexual assault. Current estimates indicate that as many as one out of nine woman students is a victim of date rape and one in five is sexually assaulted at some time during their years in University. Similar figures are found among women not attending University or College. These figures are estimates. Most date rapes and assaults are not reported, so social scientists can only make an educated guess regarding the total number based on reported cases. Many contend that these estimates are far too high; others believe the actual figures may be even higher!

These reported date rapes and assaults are not attacks carried out by some unknown assailant who comes out of the bushes, but are attacks that take place during a date by a person who is known by the victim, oftentimes well known. These assaults, with few exceptions, are carried out by men against women. There are many scenarios. Sometimes, a young woman is plied with drink at a party and her escort "takes advantage" of her. In some cases, a young man, after a period of heavy sexual petting, is unwilling to take "no" for an answer and forces himself upon her. In others, the man psychologically coerces the woman into sex by making her feel sexually inhibited, repressed or inadequate. In the majority of cases, the woman does not report the incident. The shock of the ordeal, the unwillingness to betray a "friend," the lack of awareness that the assault was a crime, or the reluctance to go public and suffer further humiliation in a courtroom are some of the main reasons why she is so reluctant to come forward.

Date rapes and assaults are not new; they have been around for a long time. However, only during the last few years has the public been made aware of the high incidence of this crime. Whether the number of occurrences has actually increased over the previous generation is hard to know because of inadequate reporting both in the past and the present. In this sexually permissive era, I suspect that the occurrence has increased. Nowadays, it is much harder for a woman to say "no" to a man. In the period before "the pill," a woman could always argue that she might get pregnant, cite religious reasons or claim the support of the majority for her decision to refrain from sex. Nowadays, these arguments no longer have the same weight. For a woman to say "no" is much more a personal rejection and, unfortunately, some men, influenced by heavy social and peer pressures, are simply unwilling to take that answer.

I have known many young women who were raped or assaulted while on a date. It was a horrible experience for them. Their pain at being betrayed and violated by a friend is immeasurable and long lasting. Many are afraid to date again. Some hate men for a long time. All of them need time and much loving support to recover their self-esteem and to regain the trust needed to relate with men once more.

Most young men respect the women they date and will not make unwanted sexual advances. Unfortunately, there are a minority who will take advantage of an unsuspecting woman. As a woman, if you do not know your date well, it makes sense to confine your dating activity to public places or to go on group dates. It is also prudent not to have too much to drink and to bring along enough money to take a taxi home. Should the need arise, make clear the parameters of the sexual activity, if any, that you are willing to engage in at that time. Simple remarks like: "I'm sorry, but I don't do behavior X on first dates," or "I don't feel comfortable engaging in X actions at this time," may be sufficient. Depending on the situation, further amplification may be necessary, either on this occasion or in time. *Leave no doubt about your sexual intentions and where you draw the line!*

As a man, it is important to appreciate that when a woman says "no" to sexual activity, she means "no!" This is just as true whether she says this on the first date or after going out with her for two years. You have no right to touch or feel her body without her consent. Her body is her body. She alone determines whether she wants to engage in sexual activity. If you are in doubt about her intentions, ask! If she does not want to relate sexually with you at this time, it is unacceptable to badger her or to try to break her will through psychological warfare. There is room for some gentle coaxing, but when it becomes clear that she means "no," then her wishes must be respected and you must control your sexual urges.

Sex is not loving when it is forced or done out of fear or intimidation. Love must be freely given; so too must the sexual expression of love.

Responsible sex and STDs

The increased sexual activity among young people in recent years, though allowing a more physically intimate relationship, has not been without its problems. The most publicized concern has been the high incidence of sexually transmitted diseases (STDs), especially AIDS.

There are over fifty different diseases that are contracted primarily through sexual contact. Each has its own cause, symptoms and form of treatment. These diseases can be painful and, if left untreated, can have serious physical consequences, like sterility or even death. They are passed on to loved ones through sexual contact and can be transmitted to unborn children and infants.

Unfortunately, despite improved medical techniques and new antibiotics, the incidence of sexually transmitted diseases continues to grow within North American society. Incomplete reporting prevents health authorities from knowing exactly how many new cases are contracted each year, but a reasonable estimate is that one out of ten sexually active persons in the United States will be infected with an STD during the next year. Reporting is incomplete because symptoms do not appear immediately in all cases, are often unrecognized or are initially so mild that persons do not bother to report them. Many persons are too embarrassed to go to a doctor or a clinic, or simply do not want to report all of their sexual partners as is required in STD cases.

The most well known sexually transmitted diseases are gonorrhea, syphilis, chlamydia, genital warts, genital herpes, and AIDS. Gonorrhea, syphilis and chlamydia are bacterial infections transmitted almost exclusively through sexual contact between adults or during the birthing process from mother to baby. They can be treated successfully in most cases with antibiotics. Genital warts, genital herpes and AIDS are caused by viruses. Since antibiotics do not kill viruses, these diseases are more difficult to treat. As yet, no cures have been found for herpes or AIDS.

Gonorrhea has existed for a long time and continues to plague North Americans. It is estimated that there is somewhere between seven hundred fifty thousand and two million new cases of gonorrhea in the U.S. each year. About 80% of women have no apparent initial symptoms, but if the disease is left untreated, the infection can cause pelvic inflammatory disease (PID), sterility and an increase in dangerous ectopic pregnancies. Men usually experience a sharp burning pain during urination shortly after becoming infected. The symptoms normally go away after two or three weeks, but the disease still exists and is contagious. Left untreated, it can cause infection of the testicles and sterility. Gonorrhea can be treated successfully in most cases through antibiotics.

Syphilis has plagued the Western world for a long time. Regrettably, despite the availability of effective treatment by anti-biotics, one hundred and thirty thousand cases still occur each year in the U.S. and the number is increasing. Without treatment, the disease can eventually lead to paralysis, severe psychiatric illness and death.

Chlamydia is rampant in the U.S. It is estimated that over four million persons are infected each year. The disease infects the urinary and reproductive tracts, and if left untreated can result in PID in women and sterility in both women and men. Unfortunately, there are often no outward symptoms of the disease, especially in women, which means that serious damage has usually been done before detection. Like gonorrhea and syphilis, chlamydia can be treated by antibiotics.

Genital warts are caused by the human papillomavirus (HPV). It is estimated that over twelve million persons in the U.S. are presently infected by this virus, with a million new cases occurring annually. The majority show no external symptoms. Others have visible warts in a variety of shapes and sizes. Some are so small that they can hardly be seen. Men get them on the penis, scrotum, anus, and inside the urethra. Women have them on the vulva, inner and outer vaginal lips, anus, inside the vagina, and on the cervix. These warts are not usually painful. Sexual contact with them is highly contagious and sex should be avoided until they are entirely removed. Long thought to be more of an embarrassment or annoy-ance than a danger, recent research indicates that HPV infection is associated with higher incidences of genital cancers in both men and women, and with cervical cancer in women. As a virus, HPV cannot be killed by antibiotics. Instead, a variety of treatments are used, including the application of ointments to the warts, alpha-inter-feron injections, laser surgery, cauterizing, or freezing. A single treatment may not be sufficient to eradicate the warts.

Genital herpes is caused by the herpes simplex virus, type 2 (HSV-2), but can also be caused by the herpes simplex virus, type 1 (HSV-1), which normally infects the mouth but can infect the genital area as well. These viruses are transmitted primarily through genital, anal or oral sexual contact. Although there is a general consensus that the incidence of genital herpes is increasing, the extent of the disease is unknown because reporting is once again inadequate. It is estimated that thirty million persons carry the virus with five hundred thousand individuals developing new cases of active genital herpes each year. The initial outbreak of genital herpes, called the primary infection, is usually the most severe. Painful blisters develop on the genitals or elsewhere. Most persons also develop flu-like symptoms, such as fever, headache and muscle pains. These symptoms usually do not go away for two or three weeks. After the initial attack, the viruses become latent and are no longer infectious. However, they can become active again at any time and cause recurrent infections. About 90% of those infected have recurring attacks and 50% of them have five or more attacks a year. Usually the recurring infections are milder. To prevent the transmission of the disease, sexual intercourse should be avoided as long as open genital sores are present. Unfortunately, there is no cure for genital herpes. Acyclovir, taken orally, can reduce the severity of the primary infection and can decrease the number of recurrent infections, but it cannot entirely eliminate the disease.

In recent years, there has been much talk about the fatal disease, Acquired Immune Deficiency Syndrome or AIDS. The great majority of researchers believe that the Human Immunodeficiency Virus (HIV), either acting by itself or in conjunction with micro-organisms known as mycoplasmas, triggers the onslaught of this terrible disease. HIV is transmitted through homosexual or hetero-sexual relations, exposure to infected blood or hypodermic needles, or by an infected mother to her fetus during pregnancy or to her newborn through breastfeeding. The presence of another STD with open sores or lesions makes it easier for the AIDS virus to be passed from one person to another during sexual intercourse. Once present, the virus will eventually attack the body's immune system to such an extent that it is unable to defend the body against the virus or other disease organisms. As a result, diseases that would normally not be life threatening become killers.

The initial stage of the infection is usually mild with few or no symptoms. Some persons do get swollen glands in various areas of the body. The virus then becomes latent for roughly seven to twelve years, only to reappear in a deadly manner. The onset of AIDS is indicated by a variety of symptoms, including weight loss, diarrhea, long term fevers, and/or the appearance of diseases like shingles. Shortly thereafter, the person will fall prey to any one of a number of infectious diseases, tumors, nervous disorders, or physical ail-ments. Once AIDS is diagnosed, most victims die within two or three years. It is not known what percentage of HIV carriers will eventu-ally get AIDS. Estimates run from 30% to 100%.

132,540 persons in the U.S. were diagnosed as having AIDS as of April, 1990. Between one and one and a half million people are presently carriers of HIV.[1] Although AIDS was originally found in North America mainly among homosexuals and intravenous drug users, recent research indicates that approximately seven per cent of new cases are being spread through heterosexual transmission, with the indication that these numbers will increase in the future. Transmission of the disease from an infected man to an uninfected woman is significantly higher than the other way around. In fact, there is only a small possibility of an infected woman passing the disease on to a man, but it happens, as "Magic" Johnson can attest. There is no cure for the HIV infection and AIDS. New treatments can help to prolong an HIV infected person's life and make him or her more comfortable during the final stages, but they cannot destroy the deadly virus.

Given the high incidence of sexually transmitted diseases, it clearly makes sense to take responsibility for ensuring that neither you nor your partner will get an unwanted sexual infection. In recent years, particularly in response to the AIDS crisis, a major health campaign has been mounted to get individuals to practice "safe sex." Central to this campaign is the use of a latex condom whenever sexual intercourse takes place. Although using a latex condom, especially in conjunction with a spermicide like octoxynol or nonoxynol-9 which provide additional protection against sexual disease organisms, can make sex *safer*, it can never make sex *entirely safe*. Condoms occasionally break. A recent *Consumer's Report*[2] questionaire of couples who regularly use condoms discovered that one couple in four experienced at least one broken condom during the year, and nearly one in eight experienced two. Overall, they calculate that one condom in 105 broke during anal intercourse and one in 165 broke during vaginal intercourse. Condoms are also ineffective if they do not cover infected areas. For example, if a man has open sores on his scrotum, a condom will not prevent infectious contact with his partner. Furthermore, if a man is not careful in taking off a condom after intercourse, contact with infected areas or with infected semen can occur. Using a condom is much better than nothing, but it is an illusion to think that it will provide total safety. If a person really wants to practice "safe sex," the only way to do it is to be sexually abstinent.

Being sexually promiscuous nowadays is like playing Russian roulette. The more sexual partners, the greater the risk of becoming infected with an STD. Bear in mind that a sexually active person may show no sympoms of a sexual infection but may still be an infectious carrier of a disease. Using condoms can make sex safer but cannot reduce the risk entirely. Not using condoms at all is foolhardy and extremely dangerous.

If you are a sexually active person and discover any genital infections or sores, or have any reason to believe that you or one of your sexual partners may be infected with an STD, contact your doctor immediately. If you are embarrassed or reluctant to communicate with your family doctor, go to a local clinic. Sexually transmitted diseases cannot be taken lightly. They should be treated immediately.

The best way to ensure that you do not get a sexually transmitted disease is to abstain altogether from sexual relations. Failing that, it is to have sex only within a mutually exclusive relationship. If neither of you have had sexual relations before, there is normally no risk of getting an STD. However, if one or both of you have had sexual relations with persons known or suspected to have had other sexual partners, then a clear risk exists. You can minimize this risk by using a condom during sex, but you cannot eliminate it. If you want real peace of mind, it is best to refrain from sexual relations until the sexually active partner(s) are tested and shown to be clear of STDs. Testing is prudent even though no symptoms of an STD may be evident, since a silent or latent infection may be present. If you or your partner test positive, sexual relations, even with a latex condom and the nonoxynol-9 spermicide, will always have some risk of passing on the infection.

Responsible sex and pregnancy

A second common problem in this age of increased sexual activity is the high incidence of premarital pregnancy. Ironically, at a time when the availability of good contraceptives has never been greater, the frequency of premarital pregnancies each year among sexually active women in North America between the ages of 15 and 24 is approximately one in ten. This figure is reached by adding the total number of unwed pregnancies, abortions of single women and marriages contracted when pregnant within an age group and dividing it by the estimated total number of unmarried sexually active women in that group. The figure is roughly the same whether the women are under or over twenty years old.

Most persons are startled when they read these numbers. They believe the ratio is closer to one in fifty or one in a hundred. A contraceptive mentality pervades most people's minds nowadays that assumes the advent of modern contraceptives has made premarital pregnancy rare, happening mainly to young teenagers. Regrettably, this is not the case. Good contraceptives are readily available but they are often misused or not used at all. The results are predictable.

A contraceptive method's theoretical reliability is based on its lowest expected failure rate. This rate is an educated guess of experts in the field, based on their collective experience and review of the literature. It is an estimate of the number of pregnancies that will happen during the course of a year to one hundred users who begin the year using the method and use it *correctly* and *consistently* throughout the year. For example, the combined birth control pills have a 0.1% lowest expected failure rate. This means that if a hundred sexually active women were to use the pill correctly and consistently for a year, less than one per cent would get pregnant. The lowest expected failure rate in this instance assumes that the women take their pills regularly, without missing a day, and use them unfailingly throughout the year. The lowest expected failure rates of most contemporary contraceptives are quite low: combined pills 0.1%; Progestogen only pills 0.5%, Norplant implants 0.03%, Depo-Provera injections 0.3%; IUDs 0.8-2%; condoms 2%; diaphragm with spermicide 6%; spermicidal foams, creams and jellies used alone 3%; sponge with spermicide 6-9%; and natural family planning methods 1-9%.[3]

Two points need to be made about these lowest expected failure rates. First, if the failure rate of a method is two per cent, it does not mean that a couple have a two per cent chance of getting pregnant the next time they have sex together. A woman is usually more fertile during the middle of her monthly cycle than at the end. Therefore, failure of a method, like a condom or a diaphragm, during the middle of the cycle may have a high likelihood of pregnancy, whereas failure at the end of the cycle may have no risk at all. The two per cent figure refers to the number of women out of one hundred who will get pregnant over the course of the year using the method correctly and consistently. Secondly, even when used correctly and consistently, these methods are not foolproof; *some women will get pregnant*. This fact must be taken into account when using them.

A better measure of the effectiveness of a contraceptive method, and a more reliable guide for most couples, is the typical failure rate. It is based on the number of pregnancies that *actually* occur during the course of a year to one hundred *typical* users who start out the year using a particular method. The typical failure rate is much higher because most couples do not always use a method correctly and consistently. For example, a woman may forget to take a pill one or two days a month; a man may not be careful in removing a condom and allows semen to spill on the woman's vulva; or a couple using a natural family planning method may gamble on having sex on a day when they should be abstinent. Typical failure rates for most contraceptive methods are much higher: combined pills 3%; progestogen only pills 3%; Norplant implants 0.03%; Depo-Provera injections 0.3%; IUDs 3%, condoms 12%; diaphragm with spermicide 18%; spermicidal foams, creams and jellies 21%; sponge with spermicide 18-28%; and natural family planning methods 20%.[4] Using no method at all will typically result in a 85% chance of pregnancy during the year.[5]

These high typical failure rates are not caused by "accidents" or "bad luck" but are primarily a matter of using these methods carelessly. Young persons, in particular, frequently fail to realize how fertile they are and often do not exercise the caution they should in using a method. Failure rates tend to decline as persons get older.

Some couples, especially younger ones, do not use contraceptives at all, believing that "it won't happen to me" or that sex with a contraceptive is somehow "impure" or lacks spontaneity. Casual sexual encounters are often engaged in without contraceptives, although the AIDS scare has encouraged greater condom usage. Even in ongoing relations, it sometimes happens that initial sexual relations occur spontaneously before any thought is given to pregnancy protection. In some cases, the couple may have sex several times before they finally sit down and talk about contraceptive methods. Needless to say, when contraceptives are not used, pregnancies will occur!

If you and your partner make a decision to have sexual intercourse, it is your responsibility to ensure that no unwanted pregnancy occurs. BEFORE you have intercourse, you should discuss how you intend to prevent conception from happening and what you will do should a pregnancy occur. I appreciate that discussing contraception and pregnancy before initiating sexual relations may sound a bit unromantic, but there is nothing romantic about an unwanted pregnancy. If you do not want a child, both of you must take responsibility to ensure that a pregnancy does not occur and the first step is to discuss how you propose to prevent a pregnancy from happening. Simply to assume that it won't happen is imprudent and irresponsible.

When choosing a contraceptive, the physical safety of the method must also be weighed. Norplant implants, Depo-Provera injections and the "pill," for example, are highly effective, but they have serious side effects for some women and should not be considered without consulting a doctor.

Since no existing contraceptive method is perfect, especially in its typical usage, it also makes sense to consider what you would do should a pregnancy occur. Using more reliable methods can reduce the risk, but cannot eliminate it. If the two of you are too young or are not in a position to handle an unwed pregnancy at this time, your intent to have intercourse should be seriously reconsidered! Sexual abstinence may be more prudent.

An unwed pregnancy, especially for a younger couple, is invariably an agonizing experience. Besides the initial shock of discovery and the tribulations involved in finding a solution, the couple often face the disappointment of parents and embarrassment before their friends and colleagues. The time is particularly difficult for the woman since she must carry the baby and will show the effects of the pregnancy. If her partner deserts her or is unwilling to marry, the decision about what to do with the child will fall mainly on her shoulders.

There are no easy decisions when an unwed pregnancy occurs. Abortion is not an option for many persons for religious or moral reasons. Even for those women for whom it is an option, it is usually a reluctant choice. Studies show that most women do not enjoy the experience of having an abortion. They may feel that it is the best decision in the circumstance, but it is not one that they relish making, especially if they feel that the fetus is human. A small number have serious guilt problems later.

The decision to bear the child and give it up for adoption is also difficult. An attachment between mother and child develops during the course of the pregnancy and most women find giving up the child extremely difficult. Even if they do make the decision to give up the child and are convinced that it is their best choice, there will always be nagging doubts about what kind of care the child will receive from the adoptive parents.

The choice to keep the child, with or without some assistance from the male partner, has its difficulties as well. In a great many cases, the woman may have to go to work to support her child, forcing her to quit school or curtail her academic development. Many of these women, unfortunately, wind up living below the poverty line. With a young child in tow, finding a future mate is also more problematic.

Getting married is another option. The decision to marry, however, should not be based solely on the fact that a pregnancy has occurred. Caring for the baby and getting married are two separate issues. The partners should consider marriage only if they love each other, have been going together for a goodly period of time and were previously considering marriage in the near future. Both must be willing to advance the date of their marriage and to accept the inconveniences involved, like not doing some of the things they wished to do before marriage or leaving school temporarily to support the family. To marry *simply* to give the child a marital home is a mistake. If the partners are not prepared to marry or do not really love each other, a rushed marriage will ultimately benefit neither the couple nor the child. "Shotgun" marriages do not have a high success rate.

Clearly, there are no easy choices when an unwed pregnancy occurs. It will be a difficult time for the partners, especially the woman. The decisions made at this time will often change the way one or both of the partners live for the rest of their lives.

A premarital pregnancy is not the end of the world. Many couples mature during the crisis and gain a greater appreciation of the depths of their relationship. Parents, after an initial period of shock and anger, usually come on side. In most cases, they are strongly supportive. Friends, the real ones, will also be supportive. Notwithstanding these manifestations of love and support, it makes sense to avoid the whole problem by taking every precaution, including abstinence, to ensure that pregnancy does not occur.

Early sexual involvement

Becoming overly involved with sex too early in a relationship is another potential difficulty for a couple desiring a long term union. When partners become focused on their sex life too soon, they tend to overlook or ignore other critical factors needed to develop their relation. In particular, they often do not spend enough time coming to know each other in other areas or working through difficulties that may cause problems later. Sex is such a powerful force that a couple can be seduced into thinking that they have a strong union when they do not. The result is that the pair may stay in a relationship which does not have a solid basis for growth and development.

As we have seen earlier, sexual love, alone or in combination with romantic love, is not sufficient to bind a couple in an ongoing intimate relationship. What is needed is a deeper self-giving love, and it cannot develop as long as the pair are focused primarily on their sex life. For this reason, it makes sense for the partners to exercise restraint in their early sexual activity. They are well advised to wait for their relationship to become more fully established before engaging in heavier sexual activity.

Sex in a casual context

In today's sexually permissive milieu, a number of men and women engage in sexual relations mainly for physical gratification. Although the AIDS scare has put a damper on the "casual sex" scene, there are still many individuals who seek sex mainly for fun and pleasure. Whether the sex takes place during "one night stands" or slightly more developed relationships, they are simply looking for the physical gratification of these unions, and not a more committed love relationship.

Although these persons may find "casual sex" to be satisfying for a while, sooner or later, and it may be much later, a life centered around sexual gratification usually begins to lose its appeal and becomes empty. Quite apart from the risks of STDs and premarital pregnancies, most discover that having sex for pleasure with no strings attached sounds good in theory, but in practice messy emotional complications frequently arise. Consciously or unconsciously, one or both partners are looking for more than sexual gratification. They hope that their sexual relations will lead to a deeper love and companionship. It can be painful if the other person does not call back or shows no interest in dating again. Experiencing the other's disappointment that the relationship was merely a sexual one, even though both of you agreed that it would be nothing more, is not always easy. In time, the emotional cost of these relations, the fears of STDs and pregnancy, as well as the desire to satisfy the deeper need for a closer relationship move most persons to look for sex within a larger love relationship.

"Sex for fun" is usually just a phase. In time, the great majority of unmarried persons want their sexual relations to be more meaningful and reserve them for a more serious relationship in which a mutual love is present.

Sex in a loving context

Most couples nowadays, as mentioned earlier, believe that sexual relations are appropriate when a couple are "in love." However, there is no full agreement about when a couple are sufficiently "in love" to begin having sex. Some hold that a couple can be truly "in love" after a few months or less. Others believe that a genuine committed love can only exist in a marital relationship. The majority take the position that sex is an appropriate expression of love when the couple's relationship has developed to the point where they have a strong ongoing commitment to each other.

1) Early "loving" sexual relations

Some feel that a couple can "hit it off" and have very strong feelings of affection towards one another within a month or two. They are indeed "in love" and sex is a legitimate way of expressing their mutual affection. Undoubtedly, contemporary films and television shows have encouraged this view by regularly depicting partners "sleeping" with each other soon after they meet.

When a couple justify sexual relations within a month or two on the grounds that they are "in love," the obvious question is what do they mean by "love?" After so short a period of time, in most cases their primary attraction is romantic and/or sexual. If the bond is mainly romantic, then the relationship is based on highly volatile feelings that come and go. There is a very real chance that when they see through their romantic haze and come to know each other better, they will not like one another and will part. Sex in their relationship may be thrilling and emotionally gratifying but it is not usually an expression of an enduring love. If the attraction is mainly sexual, even though their sex may be intensely satisfying, their relationship is based once more on feelings that may not last. When the passion subsides, the couple may discover that they do not have much else in common.

Few relationships of a month or two involve a long term commitment. More often than not, the partners have barely begun to discuss their future together. They may have good feelings about each other but in most cases they are not ready to make a lasting commitment. Their commitment is for the time being, not for a long time or forever. Since the couple have only a limited commitment to each other, their sexual relating can at best express their temporary feelings, not an abiding love!

Sex, then, in a newly formed relationship, even though it may be highly pleasurable, in most cases is not an expression of a deeper self-giving love. There is nothing particularly special about having sex when the main attraction is only a passing fancy or a sexual release. If a couple want their sexual relations to be expressive of a deeper and abiding love for each other, it makes sense for them to wait until their relationship is much more developed.

2) Waiting until marriage

At the other end of the spectrum, there are those who hold that a couple do not have a full and committed love until they are married. Sexual intercourse is a special act that expresses their deep and abiding mutual love and fidelity. As such, it should be reserved until the couple are married. As long as the pair are not married, there is always the possibility that they may separate. If they engaged in sex prior to the break up, then their sexual relating would no longer be a special expression of their personal love. The exclusive nature of sexual intercourse can be assured only if both partners practice sexual abstinence before marriage.

Waiting until marriage is also the only sure way of avoiding the risks of sexually transmitted diseases and unplanned pregnancies. In an era when "safe sex" is not safe enough and premarital pregnancy rates are high, sexual abstinence is the best way to avoid these unwanted complications. The AIDS scare and the growing number of date assaults have made more individuals reconsider the merits of waiting until marriage. The "old fashioned" way has suddenly become fashionable again!

Premarital sexual abstinence is difficult in today's sexually permissive atmosphere. The late age at which couples marry nowadays adds to the challenge. However, many unmarried couples have done it in the past and there is no reason to believe that those modern couples who set their minds to it cannot do the same today. Their sexual control may also turn out to be an asset later on in the marriage when long periods of absence or illness may require extended periods of abstinence.

Another potential problem is that sexual abstinence can sometimes cover up the sexual incompatibility of a couple. Differences over sexual frequency or personal aversions to non-traditional forms of sex may not be discovered if the couple wait until marriage. A former student of mine and her boyfriend chose to abstain from sex before marriage, only to discover afterwards that he had a strong psychological aversion to having sexual intercourse. He could engage in petting and necking, but not coitus. Although the marriage was later annulled, it was a shattering experience for her. In most cases, a couple can determine from their non-coital sex play and conversations whether a potential sex problem exists, but not always. After the pair marry, sometimes a sex therapist can help them, but not in all cases.

Sexual compatibility is a nebulous reality. A couple cannot always determine whether they will be sexually compatible during their marital years on the basis of their premarital sex. I have known several couples who had great sex before marriage, but when their marital relationship soured, so too did their sex life. I have also met couples whose sex was poor prior to marriage, mainly because one or both were uncomfortable with the circumstances of their premarital sexual activity or had moral or religious qualms. Later, after they were married, their sex life was fine. Sexual relating is not simply a physiological reality; it is psycho-physical. When partners are comfortable with each other, their own sexuality and what is going on in their lives, they will usually have good sex together. When they are not, their sex lives will often be troubled. Since these factors vary over time, so too will their compatibility.

The argument that sexual celibacy often leads to serious psychological problems is a myth. There is no scientific proof to support this position.[6] I know many celibate persons, and only a very few have had serious personal difficulties related to their sexual abstinence.

3) Sex in a committed relationship

A third position is taken by those who hold that sex is a special act that should express a deep love, but not necessarily a marital love. They believe that sexual relations should be reserved at least until the couple have a strongly committed or engaged relationship. A couple should not rush into sexual relations, but should wait for several months to a year, longer if they are younger, before becoming sexually active. By waiting, they do not allow their passions to cloud their relationship and they minimize the risks of STDs and premarital pregnancy.

In this view, sexual intercourse is seen as a natural and appropriate expression of their deep mutual love. Although there are risks involved in having premarital sex, the risks are outweighed by the positive benefits of having regular sexual intercourse. Besides, if the couple are responsible in using contraceptives, the dangers can be minimized. Should any problems arise because of their sexual involvement, their mutual commitment should see them through the difficulties.

When a couple decides not to wait until marriage, they acknowledge, at least implicitly, that their sexual relations may not be reserved exclusively for their eventual marital partner. Hopefully, they will, but since it is not uncommon for persons to have several serious relationships before they marry, sex may be had with several persons before marriage. In effect, sex becomes an exclusive expression of love but only while the couple are going together.

Deciding about sexual relating

I come from a background where couples waited until marriage before having sexual relations. I still see much merit in that position. Sex is kept as a special and exclusive expression of the couple's mutual love. Problems of sexually transmitted diseases and premarital pregnancies are avoided. The sexual control learned before marriage can often be helpful during times of separation and illness. However, if a couple cannot wait until marriage, then I would encourage them to wait as long as possible so that their sexual passion will not cloud their true marital compatibility.

My caution in these matters stems from numerous counselling sessions and conversations with couples who have had bad experiences with premarital sexual relating. I have been exposed to the pain and suffering caused by unwed pregnancies, date assaults, sexual seductions, and sexually transmitted diseases. I have also watched once healthy young men die of AIDS. The sexual revolution has freed this generation from many of the unhappy repressions of the past, but it has brought its own problems. In looking at the risks, I think couples are better to err on the side of caution.

However, when all is said and done, you and your partner must determine for yourselves what kind of premarital sexual expression is appropriate for your relationship. You must decide at what point sex is a genuine expression of your love for each other. Your decision should not be based simply on the passions of the moment, what "everyone else is doing" or what the media presents as normal. Rather it should be a thoughtful choice that weighs carefully the risks and benefits of sexual relating in your circumstances at this time. The decision should also respect your mutual personal, moral and religious convictions. In the end, you have to be responsible for your life together; no one else can be.

Concluding remarks

We are sexual beings. It is natural for us to want to relate sexually. Although our sexual urgings are physiologically based, we are not compelled like the animals to respond to hormonal and sensory cues. Instead, our minds can determine how we react to these urgings. We can choose to restrain our sexual passions or to let them have full rein. Although control can sometimes be difficult, we do not have to be slaves to our passions.

As a human activity that falls under conscious control, sexual relating within a partnership should be guided by the larger norms that govern all interpersonal relations between men and women. That is to say, these acts should be knowledgeable, respectful, non-coercive, responsible, and, most of all, loving. When sexual relations cease to follow these norms, they can be abusive and destructive. The high incidences of sexual assault, date rape, unwed pregnancies, and sexually transmitted diseases make this abundantly clear.

If you and your partner want your sexual relating to strengthen rather than hinder your union, you must make every effort to ensure that it takes place in a genuine context of love. Sexual relating is not the same as loving. It becomes loving when it responsibly expresses the deep concern that the two of you have for each other.

DISCUSSION QUESTIONS

1. Are you and your partner knowledgeable about sexual matters?
2. Are you comfortable talking with each other about sexual matters? If not, why not?
3. Do you respect your partner's right to say "no" to sexual relations?
4. Do you believe in premarital intercourse?
5. At what point in a relationship do you think sexual relations are appropriate?
6. If you are in favor of premarital sexual relations, what precautions will you take to prevent pregnancy?
7. If pregnancy occurs, what will you and your partner do?
8. If either of you has been sexually active prior to your present relationship, are you sure that you do not have an STD? Are you willing to be tested?
9. If you decide to wait until marriage, can you both exercise the sexual control needed?

CHAPTER FOURTEEN

LIVING TOGETHER

In recent years, many couples have taken to living together instead of marrying. They share a single residence on a regular and ongoing basis, and live more or less like a married couple, but they choose not to get married legally. Although the couple normally share living expenses and the upkeep of their domicile, they are more than roommates. They plan their lives around each other and are usually sexually intimate. In most cases, they have a fairly strong commitment to each other but are not necessarily committed to marriage in the future.

The phenomenon of living together in North America has increased sharply during the last twenty-five years. According to U.S. Bureau of Census statistics, the number of cohabiting American couples has grown from 450,000 in 1960 to over 2,000,000 in 1985. This constitutes about five per cent of all couples. Canadian figures are similar.[1] In Scandanavian countries like Sweden and Denmark, approximately fifteen per cent of all couples are cohabiting.[2] The practice has especially caught on among young people. A recent U. S. study indicates that approximately twelve per cent of unmarried women between the ages of 20 and 29 are presently cohabiting and roughly thirty per cent have cohabited at some time during their lives.[3] Every indication is that the numbers will continue to grow in the future.

Many factors have contributed to the rise in the number of couples living together, including the contemporary disillusionment with the ideal of marriage and the lessening of traditional marital supports. A major stimulus has been the greater sexual freedom of our western society. With the development of highly reliable contraceptive devices and their popular acceptance, unmarried couples, less fearful of pregnancy, have increasingly engaged in sexual intercourse. Over time, as attitudes regarding premarital sex have become more liberal, Universities, Colleges, apartment houses, hotels, and motels have also become less willing to chaperone people's sex lives. What a couple does in the privacy of the bedroom is their business. As soon as sex was no longer viewed as restricted to marriage and chaperonage of unmarried adult sexual liaisons became minimal, it was just a matter of time before a growing number of unmarried partners would begin to share living quarters. As more couples cohabited and found their experiences to be satisfactory, the phenomenon has gained increased popularity.

Some basic advantages of living together

Although there are many different types of living together, several basic advantages are common to most of them. Perhaps the most significant is that it allows a couple to be more personally and sexually intimate. By cohabiting, the pair can share their day to day lives more fully. Their greater physical proximity gives them more opportunity to explore their relationship and to express their mutual love and affection. They can engage in sexual relations more regularly.

Living together can also be convenient and economically advantageous. When a couple reside in the same apartment or house, they are not restricted to seeing each other only during dating times nor do they have to travel back and forth to separate residences afterwards. Economically, couples with limited funds can save money by having to pay only one rent. They can also pool their resources and share expenses.

At a time when marriage breakdown is so prevalent, cohabiting can be seen as a way for a couple to "try out" a relationship before they marry. Living in the same household on an ongoing basis can help the partners to determine more realistically their ability to live together. In particular, it will give them a chance to become more aware of each other's personal habits and to determine whether they can adapt to them. Can she live with his loud snoring at night? Can he handle her taking over an hour in the bathroom every morning? Can they mutually live with their differing standards of neatness around the house? These trivial matters may be the source of real friction in a relationship. The couple's ability, or inability, to handle them may be a foretaste of whether they can deal with more difficult problems. Learning these things before marriage can help the couple to determine whether they will be able live in a permanent relation.

Some basic drawbacks of living together

Along with these advantages, there are also several common disadvantages of living together. Parental or familial disapproval is a major problem, especially among younger cohabitants. Openly living together is a public statement that a couple are sleeping together and only a minority of parents, and even fewer grandparents, find this behavior acceptable. Most disapprove for moral or religious reasons, although the loss of face within their community is also a strong factor. Some parents disapprove of their children's actions but reluctantly tolerate their behavior. In many instances, they simply "look the other way." Others accept the couple's cohabitation but not without trying to lay a heavy "guilt trip" on them. Still others simply disown the pair, sometimes permanently. Among my younger students, the greatest deterrent to living together is the fear of parental rejection. Parental disapproval is usually less of a problem for couples who are in their mid-twenties or older. Although parents may still disapprove, they are more willing to accept their progeny's actions because they see them as adults and independent. "They are old enough to know what they are doing!" may be the response.

Disapproval of friends, employers and religious groups is a second disadvantage. As time goes by and living together becomes more acceptable, there will undoubtedly be greater tolerance within the community and among some of the Churches. However, at present, there are still strong pockets of disapproval. Reckoning with them may not always be easy.

Another common problem is an unwanted or unexpected pregnancy. Although most cohabiting couples use birth control, contraceptive failures still happen. Couples who live together are two to three times more likely to have a premarital birth than couples who do not cohabit. Some of these children were conceived prior to living together; others were conceived during the cohabitation period.[4] Coping with the problems of such a pregnancy, as we have seen, is never easy. Keeping the child, giving it up for adoption, having an abortion, or getting married sooner than planned are all difficult and anxious choices that can put severe strains on a couple, especially if they are not committed to getting married at this time.

Differing types of "living together"

So far, we have been discussing "living together" in general terms. However, the phrase "living together" is ambiguous and signifies a variety of differing ways of cohabiting. All cohabitors do not live together for the same reasons nor do they have the same degree of commitment. What can be affirmed about one cohabiting couple cannot easily be said of another. For the sake of greater clarity, then, let us differentiate six distinctive ways in which couples live together and discuss some of their particular pros and cons. Bear in mind that the differences between one type and another are not always easily distinguishable and sometimes become blurred over the course of a couple's relationship.

1) "Going steady" living together

A common type of living together is a modern day form of "going steady." The couple move in together relatively soon after they begin seeing each other. In some cases, this can happen within weeks after they start going out together. The partners are attracted to each other and want a closer relationship. In most cases, sexual desire, romantic attraction and convenience play major roles in their decision to cohabit. The couple usually have no intent to get married for the time being, although they do not rule this out in the future. They are usually committed to an exclusive relationship and to making a reasonable effort to develop their union, but they view their partnership as open-ended. In effect, they are really trying to determine if they are sufficiently compatible to consider a long term relationship. Over time, if things go well, they may consider getting married. Their union is similar to the traditional "going steady" relationship except that the couple have moved in together.

Of all the forms of living together, "going steady" cohabitation is the most chancy mainly because it is a beginning relationship. "Going steady" cohabitors, like any other couple just coming to know each other, are drawn together primarily by romantic and sexual attractions. As we have seen, these attractions, by themselves or in unison, do not provide a good foundation for a solid relationship. They tend to mask undesirable and incompatible traits. Once the romantic haze and the sexual passion subside, the partners oftentimes discover that they really live in different worlds and their relationship will be in trouble.

Like any other beginning relationship, there is a natural tendency for one or both individuals to be constantly on their best behavior during the early stages of their union. Given their limited knowledge of each other and the open-ended nature of their relationship, the partners often do not feel entirely secure about their union. As a result, in the continuing effort to attract one another, they put on their best face. However, as time goes by and they reveal themselves more fully, the couple will often discover that there are deep fundamental differences between them.

If the couple are young, there is the additional problem that one or both may not be ready to handle the demands of a serious relationship at this time. Their immaturity will surface sooner or later and be the source of further difficulties for the relationship.

Unfortunately, some persons cohabit for purely selfish reasons. For example, some men see living together as an easy way to get regular sex, a good cook and someone to clean the house. Some women cohabit mainly to entice an unwilling man to marry, or to get away from home. These motivations are more likely to be present in a "going steady" cohabitation because the partners do not know each other well. The masks of romance and sexual passion plus the "good behavior syndrome" often hide the exploitative designs of a person who is in a relationship mainly for ulterior motives. As time goes by, these intentions will usually be discovered but not without pain and the probable break up of the relationship.

2) "Open-ended" living together

The second type of living together is similar to the first except that the couple do not move in together until after six months or a year and their relationship has reached a more serious level. Once again, the partners have no intention to marry in the near future, but they are open to the possibility. They usually have a strong commitment to an exclusive partnership and to working at their relationship. However, they see their union as open-ended for the time being.

Since the couple begin to live together at a later stage, they have usually worked through the trials and tribulations of their beginning relationship. Their union will normally have a firmer foundation and will be more stable.

The open-endedness of the relationship, however, can eventually become a serious problem for some couples. As long as the partners are in a transitional stage in their lives, where one or both are going to school or are trying to establish themselves in a career, they will usually be contented with a strong but open-ended commitment, believing that they are not yet ready for marriage. However, once their goals are achieved and the couple get to the point where marriage is possible, sooner or later, one of the partners will become discontent with the uncertainty of their union and will press for a more permanent commitment. He or she will either want to get married or at least to receive a firm promise of marriage in the future. If the other partner is willing, there will be no problem. But if the other does not want to get married, tensions will develop that could lead to the break up of the union.

3) "Anti-marriage open-ended" living together

A third type of living together exists when a couple cohabit with the firm intention not to marry in the near or distant future. Unlike the first two types of cohabiting, there is no "wait and see" attitude. The couple definitely do not want marriage. They want to be companions and desire to share a home together. They have a fairly strong commitment to the development of their union and are usually sexually exclusive. However, the partners also want the freedom to be able to leave the relationship at any time if so desired. They do not want to feel psychologically "tied down" to each other. This form of cohabiting can develop out of the first two types of living together or it can be initiated on its own.

As we have seen, there are some persons who simply do not feel comfortable making a permanent commitment. They want companionship and sex, but, for personal, philosophical or psychological reasons, do not wish to be confined by a marriage commitment. As long as both partners are basically compatible and are at ease with their open-ended relationship, their partnership can be satisfying and can last for a long time. I have known several couples who have lived together in an open-ended relationship for well over ten years. A classic example of a long term open-ended union is the relationship between Simone de Beauvoir and Jean-Paul Sartre, the famous French writers and philosophers. They were philosophically opposed to marriage and wanted the freedom to relate with other persons of the opposite sex, but they lived together off and on in an open-ended relationship for over fifty years.

The major difficulty with this kind of arrangement is that most of us cannot handle the insecurity of a long term open-ended relationship. We may find it acceptable for a while, but over time the uncertainty of not knowing whether the other intends to stay and to work at the relationship can become profoundly unsettling. At a certain point, it is normal to want a clear assurance from our partner that he or she intends to stay. If it is not forthcoming, we will be frustrated and may leave the relationship.

Bearing and raising children is an additional problem. Although children can be raised well by one parent, most persons feel that it is better for a child to be brought up in a two parent union. An open-ended union with no future intent to marry, no matter how strong, starts with the premise that the partners have the freedom to leave the relationship if they so desire. True enough, a married couple can break up, leaving a child with only one primary parent, but at least the couple start with a serious intent to stay together. They do not see themselves as having the freedom to leave the relationship whenever they want. If the couple in an ongoing open-ended living together arrangement do decide to have children, given that the possibility of a break up is built right into the fabric of their commitment to each other, they should consider beforehand how they will care for them should their relationship end.

4) "Trial marriage" living together

A fourth type of living together is what is commonly called a "trial marriage." In this form of cohabitation, the couple move in together after their relationship has reached a serious level of development. They definitely intend to marry in the future and see their living together as a final way of testing their relationship. They have a strong commitment to each other and will break up only if a serious problem cannot be reconciled. Their living together is really the final stage of their courting process.

The primary advantage of a "trial marriage" is that it gives the couple an opportunity to live like husband and wife before they finally pronounce their vows. If there are any significant problems in the relationship, hopefully they can be discovered before the couple marry. Sometimes, by living together, the couple can recognize problems that may not be seen if they did not cohabit. Should problems arise, they can try to work them out beforehand. If the difficulties are serious, they can postpone their marriage or, if necessary, break off the relationship.

Although a "trial marriage" may allow the couple to uncover certain problems that might not be discovered except by living together, the one thing that it cannot do is enable the partners to determine what it means to live in a permanent relationship. The couple cannot "try out" marriage. They can live in the same quarters and perform similar activities as married couples, but there is no way a permanent commitment can be "tried out." As long as the couple see their relationship as open-ended, the mind set of their relationship is open-ended. Though they may live and act as if their union is forever, deep down they know that it is not and realize that they can get out of it. The only way that a couple can really know what is entailed in making a permanent marital commitment is to make one!

5) "Preceremonial" living together

Some couples who live together do not see their relationship as being open-ended. Rather, they understand themselves as already having a permanent commitment to each other. Although they have not gone through a legal wedding ceremony, they consider themselves to be effectively married. For them, a marriage does not come into being through a legal ceremony, but through the free consent of the two partners. A *legal* marriage is effected through a legal ceremony, but a marriage comes into being as soon as the couple mutually commit to a lifelong relationship with one another. Marital consent, then, normally occurs before a couple actually gets legally married. For example, they would argue that most couples are no less committed to each other two weeks before their wedding than they are after the ceremony. In effect, they are married before the ceremony.

"Preceremonial" living together can develop in a number of ways. In some instances, the relationship between a couple involved in the first, second or fourth types of cohabiting evolves to the point where their commitment to each other becomes permanent. They intend to marry legally in the future, but for the time being they are content to cohabit. In other cases, a non-cohabiting couple whose relationship has developed to the point where they consider themselves effectively married decide to move in together. Sometimes, their reasons may be purely practical, like moving in together to save money on rent. At other times, the couple may not be able to get legally married because one or both are already married and their divorces are still pending. They are permanently committed to each other and want to share a common household. This type of living together was more common in the past when divorces were more difficult to get. In some instances, the concern is a Church annulment rather than a legal divorce. For example, a previously married Catholic who is waiting for a Church decree of nullity may live together with his or her partner until such time as a religious marriage is possible. In all of these cases, the wedding ceremony simply makes public what is already privately agreed upon by the two persons.

A living together relationship that has reached the point where the couple are permanently committed is similar to a marriage but without the legal sanction and protection. If the couple have developed a strong love for each other, share many common interests and have good lines of communication, their relationship, in most cases, will be strong. However, if their commitment was made without sufficient preparation, then, like any other couple rushing into marriage, chances are that their union will eventually have problems.

6) "Anti-law" living together

A sixth type of living together involves a couple who have made an exclusive and permanent commitment to each other, but are unwilling to get legally married because they believe the law is unfair, irrelevant or has no business regulating what they understand to be a personal affair. To illustrate, a few years ago, two students at my University celebrated a public but non-legal wedding ceremony. They exchanged traditional vows in front of friends in a lovely outdoor setting down by the river. However, they did not marry before a justice of the peace because they believed that the marriage law at the time was especially unfair to women. They did not feel that their mutual lifelong commitment needed to be sanctioned by a "piece of paper."

The obvious advantage of an "anti-law" living together relationship is that the couple can be "married" without being subject to what they consider unfair or sexist marital laws. However, this advantage is precisely its main disadvantage: the couple lack the protection of the law should one or other partner turn out to be irresponsible or ruthless. Historically, marital laws have come into being to protect the innocent within a marriage. Ours is not the only generation in which husbands have left their wives and children and refused to pay support. Although some laws or their applications have been and continue to be unfair and biased by sexist overtones, what is needed is not the abolition of all marital laws but their reform. In recent years, most western societies have begun a process designed to bring their laws more into line with more equitable ideals of marriage.

Even if a couple choose not to get married legally, their relationship is not entirely exempt from the civil law. They are still subject to other laws that will effect property settlements as well as the support and custody of their children should their union break down. For example, in most jurisdictions, goods purchased within a cohabiting relationship will belong to the person who bought them, and the mother will probably be given custody of her children. In addition, in many locales, there are so-called "palimony" laws that govern spousal support and property distribution when partners have cohabited for a certain period of years.

If a couple are unhappy with the marriage laws, in many jurisdictions they have the option to draw up a marriage contract enabling them to effectively write their own marital law. Where this possibility is present, it may be a better option than living "common law."

Does cohabiting increase your chances to get married?

If you are ready to get married and your partner is not, is living together a good way to entice him or her into marrying you? Will the ongoing close contact make your partner more willing to marry?

Although living together in an open-ended manner enables a couple to share the same residence, the same bed and much of their lives, their closeness will not necessarily make them want to spend the rest of their lives together. Their cohabiting will probably help them to gain a deeper appreciation of each other and this may lead to an eventual marriage. However, obtaining a better knowledge and developing a deeper concern for the other do not necessarily translate into a desire for a lifelong union. Other factors, like being financially or emotionally unprepared to get married at this time may be more significant and may keep one or both of the partners from making a marital commitment.

In some cases, living like a married couple without being married may actually diminish the urgency of the reluctant partner to "tie the knot." For example, If a young man can get regular sex and someone to cook the meals and do the laundry, he will be in no rush to get married. Why change a good thing!

Using living together as a scheme to entice your partner into marriage is a risky venture for both of you. If your partner is not ready to marry, putting undue pressure on him or her while cohabiting will invariably cause resentment and arguments. Even if the marriage does come about, if your partner felt pressured into the union, sooner or later, he or she will resent what happened and may want out of the relationship. Pushing a person into an unwanted marriage defeats the whole idea of having a marriage based on a free self-giving love.

Does cohabiting make for better marriages?

If you choose to live together with your partner and eventually decide to get married, will cohabiting make for a better marriage?

Advocates of living together, going back to the influential philosopher Bertrand Russell at the beginning of this century, have consistently argued that cohabiting before marriage will make for better marriages. They contend that incompatible couples will eventually break up, leaving the best couples to get married. This hypothesis was not able to be seriously tested in the past because few people actually cohabited. Only the very rich, movie stars and the very poor were willing to defy convention. The great majority were discouraged by social and economic pressures. However, times have changed, and the number of cohabiting couples has grown steadily during the past twenty-five years. It is now possible to inquire into their marital success rates as compared to a similar group who did not cohabit. Several significant studies of American, Canadian and Swedish cohabitors have been done in the past decade.

Surprisingly, almost all of the recent studies show that cohabitors who later marry had *significantly higher* rates of divorce than comparable couples who married but did not cohabit.[5] Balakrishnan *et al*, based on the 1984 Canadian Fertility Survey, reported that Canadian cohabitors were fifty per cent more likely to divorce than non-cohabitors.[6] Bennett, Blanc and Bloom, drawing upon a 1981 Swedish study, found that cohabiting Swedish women had an eighty per cent greater likelihood of getting divorced.[7] Teachman and Polonko, using a 1986 U.S. longitudinal study of 1972 High School graduates, discovered that after ten years, cohabiting women were twenty-one per cent more liable to divorce than non-cohabitors and cohabiting men were fifty-six per cent more likely.[8] Other studies also showed that they had significantly lower rates of marital satisfaction and poorer levels of communication.[9] Contemporary researchers did not expect these results. They had presumed, like those before them, that cohabitation would have pruned out the poor relationships and left the good ones.

Why do cohabitors have higher rates of divorce and marital instability than comparable couples who married but did not cohabit? Researchers are not sure. Part of the problem may be the fact that the present studies have not adequately probed the background of cohabitants or their reasons for living together. More research clearly needs to be done. For now, researchers can only speculate why cohabitants have been less successful in their marriages.

Some suggest that cohabitation itself may be the main cause of marital dissatisfaction and divorce.[10] By living together, a couple learn to think in terms of an open-ended union rather than a permanent relationship and this may make them more prone to divorce when the going gets rough. Also, in some cases, guilt feelings or strained relations with parents arising from the cohabitation may cause problems for a pair after they are married.

Although this hypothesis may have some truth, no conclusive evidence has been found so far to support the claim that cohabitors learn to think in terms of an open-ended union through living together.[11] Furthermore, studies show that the great majority of persons who cohabit have no regrets at doing so. They do not usually carry guilt into their marriages.[12]

A second theory is the "accelerated marriage" hypothesis. Studies have consistently shown that the longer a couple have been married, the greater the likelihood their marriage will eventually end in divorce. If the duration of a cohabiting couple's relationship is measured from the time they began cohabiting, rather than from the time they got married, and is compared to the length of time a non-cohabiting couple have actually been married, the results tend to be similar. In other words, the reason for the higher divorce rates of cohabiting couples is simply a matter of having lived together as "married" for a longer time than comparable couples who did not cohabit.[13]

Although the length of time a couple has lived together, whether married or unmarried, may be a consideration in bringing about the breakdown of their relationship, it is not the only factor, nor is it necessarily the most important one. The study by Bennett, Blanc and Bloom has shown that other considerations, like the presence of a premaritally conceived child or young age at the time of marriage, are better predictors of whether a marriage between cohabitors will remain intact.[14]

A third alternative is that cohabitors as a group include more persons who are less committed to marriage and are not good marriage material. Studies have shown that cohabiters in general tend to be less religious. They have lower rates of Church attendance and are more likely not to have any religious faith.[15] As such, they are more likely to disregard traditional religious teachings opposed to divorce. The studies have also shown that a disproportionate number of cohabitors come from broken homes.[16] These persons are more likely to have negative feelings about lifelong marriage. Cohabitants have also been shown to be more willing to engage in unconventional behavior. They are sexually active at a younger age and more apt to have a child out of wedlock. They get into trouble more often with the law and are more liable to use drugs. As well, cohabitors have greater trouble holding a job and tend to be less fiscally responsible.[17]

To my mind, this third alternative, which is accepted by many contemporary researchers,[18] is probably the best overall explanation for the higher incidence of marital instability and divorce among cohabitors. Given the unconventionality of living together in the late sixties and seventies, it is not surprising that a greater number of persons having more liberal values would be the first to cohabit, especially in the more open-ended styles. If and when these persons married, they would be less committed to the ideal of lifelong marriage and would be more apt to have marital difficulties due to their less conventional lifestyles.

Does cohabiting always make for poorer marriages?

Although the studies show that cohabitants who later marry are more likely to have marital difficulties and higher rates of divorce, it must not be thought that all cohabiting couples are equally at risk to have a poor marriage. The higher levels of marital breakdown and divorce among former cohabitants, as we have suggested, is most probably, but not exclusively, the result of their unconventional attitudes, lesser marital commitment and relational incompetence. Many cohabitors who later marry are committed to lifelong marriage and have fairly conventional attitudes towards life and marriage. If we exclude from consideration those couples who espouse more liberal attitudes and engage in more unconventional behavior, I suspect the marital success rates of cohabitants and noncohabitants would probably be much closer. As cohabitation becomes more popular, it is likely that more couples having conventional attitudes towards marriage and life will cohabit. This will probably mean that the association between cohabitation and marital dissolution will largely disappear in the future. The study by Schoen, showing that recent cohabitors have lower incidences of marital dissolution than older cohabitors, supports this thesis.[19]

Choosing to live in an open-ended relationship

Couples involved in one of the open-ended cohabiting arrangements have a greater possibility of not getting married, or having marital problems if they do. They have less chance of getting married because as a group they tend to be less committed to lifelong marriage, and therefore do not have as great a desire or need to be married. Couples involved in a "going steady" open-ended type of living together are particularly liable to end their relationship without getting married simply because they come to the union so poorly prepared. Their lack of knowledge about each other and what they both want from their relationship increases the probability that they will eventually discover they are incompatible.

The lack of commitment to lifelong marriage also makes those involved in an open-ended cohabitation more liable to terminate a marital relationship should they marry. This contention is supported by the Bennett, Blanc and Bloom study. It shows that couples who have been living together for three or more years, as is the case in some "open-ended" and many "anti-marriage open-ended" relationships, are much more liable to get divorced than couples who cohabit only for a short time before they get married. Those who live together for longer periods of time tend to be those who are least committed to the ideal of lifelong marriage, whereas those who live together for only a brief time before marrying are probably those who are more committed to a lasting union.[20]

If you are interested in eventually getting married to your partner, living together in an open-ended relationship is risky. Before you consider an open-ended cohabitation, it would be prudent to make sure that your partner's current desire not to marry is not a permanent aversion to marriage. As mentioned before, simply living together will not ensure that your partner will ever want to get married, and putting extra pressure on him or her to wed could well result in an unwanted and uncertain marriage.

Trial marriage versus traditional engagement

Although the studies indicate that living together in a "trial marriage" does not improve a couple's chances of having a good marriage, many persons remain skeptical, particularly those who have had positive experiences cohabiting. They are convinced that a couple preparing for marriage can learn a lot more about each other by moving in together than by residing in separate quarters and pursuing a more traditional courtship. They believe that the additional knowledge and closeness will help the partners to make a better assessment of whether they can "make it" as a married couple. The paradigm example used to support their case is the experience of friends who become roommates. They point out that two persons often get along well as friends, but when they actually share a room or an apartment, living in close quarters frequently causes major problems for them. Having a friend who is a "slob" is one thing; living with him or her is another!

It is my opinion that living together in a "trial marriage" will *not significantly* help *most* couples to have a better marriage. From my experience with engaged couples, I have come to believe that most can prepare themselves quite well for marriage without cohabiting. If the pair have been going out together for some time, they will usually spend considerable time together and see each other in a variety of situations. They spend time at one another's apartment, eat together, deal with parents and relatives, go on trips together, and meet with each other's friends. On weekends and during holidays, it is not uncommon for them to spend the bulk of their waking time together. Even though the couple do not live together, they can learn enough about each other to be able to determine quite well whether they can have a good marriage.

I grant that a couple involved in a traditional engagement will not learn as much as a cohabiting couple about some personal living habits, nor will they experience what it means to live together twenty-four hours a day on an ongoing basis. However, except in rare cases, I do not think that this information is absolutely necessary for establishing a marital relationship. If the couple have been going together for a reasonable period of time, have spent a goodly amount of time with each other and have worked at their relationship, they will usually know each other well enough to determine if they are maritally compatible.

The roommate example given above is only valid if the friends have not spent sufficient time together before moving into the same room or apartment. Sometimes, two persons may become quite friendly through playing sports, working in the same office or socializing together. However, if they have not spent much time together in other areas of their lives, when they move in together, sharp differences in the way the two live may be revealed, causing real problems. However, if the two friends have known each other for quite a while and have experienced one another in a wide variety of circumstances, they will probably not learn anything startlingly new from sharing a residence. They will usually know what to expect.

I do not wish to imply that living together in a "trial marriage" cannot be an effective way for a couple to prepare for marriage. It can be. My point is that I do not believe that it is *necessary* for a couple to live together to have a good marriage. A couple in a traditional courtship can prepare themselves just as well.

The success of any marriage depends more on whether the couple develop qualities like a vital caring love, good lines of communication, an ability to resolve conflicts constructively, a strong mutual commitment, and a shared future vision. Living together, by itself, does not ensure that a couple will develop these traits or that they will work at developing their relationship. Just because the partners reside in the same apartment and share the same bed does not mean that they will learn to communicate well or to resolve serious problems in a constructive way. Nor does it mean that they will develop a deep caring attitude and an ongoing commitment to the relationship. If simply moving into the same residence accomplished this, then the solution to every married couple's problems would be at hand! Of course, going through the traditional engagement process also does not guarantee that a couple will develop these attributes or will work at their union.

To my mind, whether a couple live together or not is not as significant as *how well* they prepare for marriage within these styles of developing a relationship. Either approach can be fruitful or inadequate.

Should you live together?

Should you and your partner live together? As we have seen, recent studies have shown that living together is not a panacea for the ills of modern marriage. Cohabiting, especially in an open-ended relationship, probably will not help you to marry your partner and will likely decrease your chances of having a good marriage. This is especially true if you move in together early in your relationship. If you live together in a more committed union, your chances of marital success will be improved but will probably be no better than if you did not cohabit. There is *no* empirical evidence that living in a "trial marriage" will increase your chances of having a more successful marriage.

Even though cohabiting, generally speaking, does not make for better marriages, there are other reasons why you and your partner may choose to live together. By cohabiting, the two of you can share your day to day lives more fully. You have the opportunity to be more personally and sexually intimate. You can learn some things about each other not possible within a traditional courtship. Sharing a single residence can save you money and is more convenient.

These benefits will have to be weighed against any moral or religious objections that either of you may have. Will you have qualms or serious guilt feelings if you cohabit? Possible parental and familial disapproval will also have to be considered. If your parents would be deeply troubled by your cohabitation, is it worth offending them just to spend more time together or to save money?

You may also decide to live together simply because you do not want to get married. You desire the closeness of day to day living but do not want to make a permanent commitment. If both of you are aware of the limits of your commitment, have not rushed into the relationship and are willing to live in an open-ended relationship, your cohabitation will probably be satisfactory, at least for awhile. As mentioned before, many persons eventually become troubled with an open-ended relationship and seek a more permanent commitment. This may cause future tensions in your relationship.

Ultimately, your decision to live together is highly personal. What is right for you will not be right for another couple. Like any other significant decision, it is important to weigh the pros and cons honestly and not allow yourself to be unduly influenced by what others are doing or by the passions of the moment. In the end, you are the ones who must live with your choice.

DISCUSSION QUESTIONS

1. Do you think that you and your partner should live together before marriage? Why?
2. Do you have moral or religious objections to living together?
3. Will your parents object to your cohabitation? How will you respond to their objections?
4. Are you prepared to live together in an open-ended way?

CHAPTER FIFTEEN

SOME FINAL THOUGHTS

The decision to get married is one of the most important of your life. If you want a lasting marriage, your decision should be weighed carefully and be based upon considerable experience together. During the early stages of your relationship, it is important for you and your partner to spend enough time with each other to determine whether you really are compatible and are willing to work together to build a lifelong union. A good lifelong union does not just happen; it needs to be lovingly created by the two of you.

Don't rush into marriage

I cannot emphasize enough the importance of not rushing this decision. All too often, I have seen couples dash into a marriage because they have fallen in love. When cupid's arrow strikes, they feel so wonderful that they cannot imagine ever having any serious problems. Arguments and fights are for other couples. Their love is special! Unfortunately, all too rapidly the real world impinges on their fanciful universe and their romantic feelings quickly subside. Ironically, within a few years, many of these same persons can no longer stand each other.

Romantic feelings are blind. They often draw persons together who really do not belong together. The initial exhilarating feelings frequently cover up the deficiencies of a partnership. That is why it is so important to take your time in forming a relationship. What appears so wonderful at the beginning may not be so hot as time passes.

Even if you have moved beyond the romantic to a more realistic view of each other, you will need time together to determine whether you are really a good match. Do you enjoy being together? Are you able to communicate effectively and to work through difficulties constructively? Do you share sufficient common interests? Can you live with each other's personal and religious values?

Working out the basic parameters of your future relationship also takes time. Where will you live? Will you both work? What are your financial priorities? Do you both want children? Do either of you have aging parents who may need care? How much involvement will you have with one another's families and friends? How will you spend your free time?

The decision to get married, like any other significant choice, should not be made in haste. Allow yourselves ample time to work through your relationship. There is no need to rush.

Spend quality time together

Throughout your courtship, to facilitate getting to know each other and to work though your marital plans, it is important to spend quality time together. By "quality time," I mean periods of time when the two of you can really share your thoughts and feelings with each other directly and honestly. Sometimes, a couple can be together a lot, but do not achieve a real meeting of minds and souls. For example, a pair can spend most of their their time together going to bars with friends. They enjoy the camaraderie of the group but they do not spend much time alone. Their social life effectively inhibits their process of coming to know one another.

Television and video watching is another common trap that prevents some couples from spending sufficient quality time together. Evenings alone revolve around watching football games, favorite TV shows or rented movies. Although the partners are together, in a very real sense they are not. Their main interest is not one another but what is on the television. Their conversations are directed mainly towards what is on the screen rather than to their life together. When television watching starts to take over your relationship, it is time to turn off the TV. It is more important to relate with each other than with Phil Donahue or Oprah Winfrey. Try going out for walk. Its healthier both for your body and your relationship.

Sometimes the culprit is sexual overinvolvement. As we have mentioned before, if your time together becomes too focused on your sexual activity, you cease to explore your relationship in a deeper way. In addition, you risk allowing your sexual feelings to deceive you into thinking that you have a strong relationship when in fact you do not. The point is not to cut off your sexual relating; it is to prevent it from dominating your relationship.

In some situations, spending so much time with friends, watching TV or engaging in sexual activity may actually be masking a deeper problem in your relationship. Perhaps, consciously or unconsciously, you are avoiding being alone together because you really have so little to say to each other. You find being by yourselves difficult and awkward. If that is so, it may be an indication that the two of you do not share enough in common to build a good relationship, or that one or both of you have a significant inability to communicate well. In either case, the problem is serious and needs to be confronted as soon as possible.

Specific preparations for your marriage

When your relationship reaches the point where you are seriously thinking about marriage, it makes sense to explore more fully what it means to be married. There are several outside resources that you can draw upon to help you in your quest. Don't be shy in using them. Marriage is an extremely complex subject. There is always more to learn.

For starters, if you have some friends who were recently married, talk to them about their married life together. You will inevitably find that they have several good insights and suggestions. Learning about their early marital experiences may help you to be more realistic in your marital expectations.

If you think that your parents or some of your relatives have good relationships, approach them about their marriages. They may be willing to share their experiences. Their lengthy time together will invariably provide you with some real wisdom.

Marriage preparation courses sponsored by Churches and community agencies, normally at little or no cost, are another good resource. Some Churches require their members or parishioners to take one. The speakers and lead couples are usually volunteers, although many are professionals. They become involved with these courses mainly because they believe in marriage and want to share their insights and experiences with young couples.

There are three basic types of programs. The first approach relies mainly on a lecture format. Married couples, doctors, lawyers, and clerics give talks on topics like communication, conflict resolution, finances, sex, the legalities of marriage, and the religious aspects of marriage. These sessions may take place over a weekend or may be stretched over several weeks. Usually, the couples will spend some time in a group discussion led by a married couple and perhaps may spend some periods alone reflecting on specific aspects of their relationship.

The second approach emphasizes discussion. Six to eight couples meet weekly with a married lead couple. Each week, for four to eight weeks, a different subject is discussed. The topics of the sessions may be determined in advance or may be decided by the participants themselves. Sometimes, specific reading or video material are assigned for the meetings. During the sessions, the couples are especially encouraged to focus on their own relationships rather than to speak in generalities.

A third approach, the engaged encounter, emphasizes personal communication between the couple. In this program, several couples come together to spend a weekend at a retreat house or some other residential location. Although there are some group sessions with two or three married lead couples, the individual couples spend most of their time by themselves. During the course of the weekend, the partners are asked to write out answers to specific questions pertaining to their relationship. They exchange their "love notes" with one another and discuss them. Although some of the questions seem irrelevant to the couple, others will often spark a deep discussion between them.

Obviously, a couple cannot expect to learn all there is to know about marriage in one weekend or several weekly sessions. However, studies have shown that couples who attend marriage preparation courses do have a slightly better success rate in their marriages than couples who do not. From my experience, I have found that the lecture and discussion sessions invariably raise some issues that a couple have not considered before. Although much of what is said by the speakers and participants simply reinforce preexisting ideas, the couple still benefit from having these ideas bolstered, especially if they are somewhat unsure about some of them.

The engaged encounter is particularly helpful for couples who have not spent much time talking with each other. During the weekend, they are forced to confront some highly personal issues on a one to one basis. In some cases, they may be unable to resolve some of their differences and may decide to postpone or even forego their marriages. This is much less likely to happen in the lecture or discussion approaches.

In my experience, I have found that the quality of marriage preparation programs varies greatly from place to place. If you are interested in attending one, it makes sense to make some exploratory investigations into their calibre. If you hear about a good one, it will usually be worth your while to attend.

Besides these Church or community sponsored courses, there are also several professional marriage preparation programs available. They are usually conducted by marriage counsellors or psychologists. The programs usually focus on the individual couple, and use sophisticated compatibility questionaires and special video presentations. Most of them are quite expensive, but the organizers claim to have high marital success rates. Given the high costs, before enrolling in one, I would suggest getting some good outside references.

A word about weddings

Nowadays, it is not uncommon for a couple to spend much of their time just prior to getting married on the wedding itself. Weddings are often elaborate affairs costing thousands of dollars. According to *Bride Magazine*, the average North American first wedding costs well in excess of ten thousand dollars. Parties that large require a lot of planning and work.

Although preparing for a wedding is usually a fun time for the couple, there are some aspects that will be tedious and emotionally upsetting. Tempers will fray and heated words will be exchanged. Inevitably the best of plans will go awry. The bridesmaids' shoes don't match their dresses! The caterer goes bankrupt! The florist can't get orange roses at this time of year! Family politics will often come into play. Aunt Martha is upset because you invited Uncle Tom's children to the wedding but not hers! Cousin Jim won't come to the wedding if his ex-wife is invited! In the end, things will usually work out. There will invariably be hitches, but hopefully, in time, you will look back upon them with amusement.

Your wedding is a special and joyous occasion. It is a celebration of your love and joining together. It is a time when your two families are united and a new family is begun. Nevertheless, it is important for you and your partner not to become so involved temporally and emotionally in your wedding preparations that you lose sight of your own relationship. The wedding is important, but even more important is your own union. Make sure that you allow yourselves sufficient quality time together during this period to enable your friendship to grow and to work through any problems that may arise in the meantime.

Hopefully, you have not decided to go forward with wedding plans if a major problem still exists between the two of you. However, if you did or a new one has arisen since you began your wedding preparations, the resolution of that problem must take precedence over your wedding plans. Should it happen that a serious impasse is reached on the issue, it makes sense to delay your wedding until the difficulty is resolved. As mentioned before, getting married, by itself, will not solve serious problems. Postponing or even calling off the wedding undoubtedly will be difficult and embarrassing. Your family will be upset. You may lose some deposits and will have to return wedding gifts. Nevertheless, this is really a small price to pay if you are really not sure about your relationship. To marry under these circumstances is to court future disaster.

Personalize your wedding ceremony

In the course of planning your wedding, don't lose sight of the fact that your exchange of vows is really the most significant part of the day. What comes afterwards is essentially a big party to celebrate what has taken place during that exchange. It makes sense, then, to put some thought into the ceremony. In particular, if you can, write your own vows. At that special moment when you commit yourselves to each other for life, do it in words that express your own thoughts rather than using someone else's words. If you are afraid that you will be too nervous to remember them at the time of the ceremony, write them out on a card and either read them or repeat them after the minister or judge.

There are many other things that you can do to particularize your ceremony, like selecting the music and the musicians, picking relevant readings, and getting friends and family members to participate in the ceremony. If you are marrying in a Church, there are some special religious rituals that both of you may find meaningful. Talk to your minister or priest about them. If there are any longstanding familial customs pertaining to the marriage ceremony, consider including them as well.

In my experience, I have found that couples who take the time to personalize their wedding ceremony, enjoy that part of the day much more than couples who do not. Their exchange of vows becomes more meaningful to them. The ceremony also sets the tone for the rest of the day. I have been at many weddings where the spirit of love and commitment expressed by the partners moved all those present and pervaded the remaining festivities.

Work at your relationship

Throughout this book, I have emphasized that the partners must *work* hard at their relationship. To work at something, be it marriage or any other task, means to make an effort, sometimes difficult, to overcome obstacles and accomplish a goal. Working at a marriage differs from other kinds of work in that its main focus is on the way a couple relate to each other. The couple need to work at developing good lines of communication, resolving conflicts satisfactorily and strengthening their mutual commitment. They will need to make a real effort at times to resolve their interpersonal difficulties.

The term "work" is commonly used to refer to a burdensome activity that we really do not care to do. Typical examples are cleaning the toilet, vacuuming the house or fixing a flat tire on a cold night. We do these activities because we have to, not particularly because we want to do them. However, the term can also be used to refer to an endeavor that is done out of love. The effort required may be difficult and even time consuming but basically it is satisfying. For instance, persons who garden as a pastime do not find it to be a burdensome activity. Even though gardening may involve hard physical labor, they enjoy what they are doing. They can't wait to get home in the evening so that they can put in a new row of flowers and enjoy the ones that are in bloom. Their love of gardening takes the burden out of their efforts. It is in this second meaning that we use the term "work" in a marriage. The partners "work at" their relationship because they love each other. Their sacrifices, compromises and restraints flow out of their mutual concern. Their work is a work of love, not a burden.

Concluding remarks

An intimate lifelong marriage is a great blessing. It is a precious gift to have a lifelong partner with whom to share your deepest thoughts and dreams; a friend, to provide ongoing counsel and support in good times and bad; a companion, to share the adventure of human existence; a mate, to build a family together. A good marriage is worth making careful preparations to bring into existence and working hard to keep.

DISCUSSION QUESTIONS

1. Do you spend enough quality time together?
2. Are your wedding plans getting in the way of your relationship?

ENDNOTES

Introduction

1. See Paul H. Landis, *Making the Most of Marriage*, 5th ed., 306-307.

Chapter One

1. This segment on romantic love is drawn in part from Dorothy Tennov's excellent book *Love and Limerence: The Experience of Being in Love*. She uses the term "limerence" to describe what I am calling "romantic love." Pages 15-81 are especially relevant.

Chapter Two

1. No single adjective can adequately describe this mode of love. I prefer the term "self-giving" because it emphasizes this love's active focus on the other. It is a love that is an active concern for the well-being and growth of the other.

2. Erich Fromm, *The Art of Loving*.

3. C.S. Lewis, *Four Loves*.

4. Rollo May, *Love and Will*.

5. Abraham Maslow, *Toward a Psychology of Being*.

6. John Powell, *Unconditional Love*.

Chapter Three

1. See Sidney B. Simon and Suzanne Simon, *Forgiveness: How to Make Peace with your Past and Get on with Your Life*, 9-21.

Chapter Seven

1. For further discussion of this topic, see David Viscott, *The Language of Feelings*.

Chapter Nine

1. For a good treatment of this topic see: George S. Bach and Peter Wyden, *The Intimate Enemy: How to Fight Fair in Love and Marriage.*

2. *Ephesians* 4, 26.

Chapter Twelve

1. I have chosen to use the phrase "dual income" rather than "dual career" because it includes both careers and jobs. The term "career" implies an occupational pursuit that is undertaken as a permanent calling, involving progressive achievement. The work is undertaken as much for personal satisfaction as for money. Professional, public and managerial positions are usually viewed as careers. In contrast, a job is work undertaken primarily to earn money rather than to gain personal satisfaction. Being a sales clerk, laborer or gasoline attendant are normally seen as jobs rather than careers. At times, the distiction between "career" and "job" can become blurred. What might be a job to one person may be a career to another.

Chapter Thirteen

1. As of August 6, 1991, there were 5246 reported cases of AIDS in Canada. Ninety per cent of the patients were male. Homosexual activity was present in eighty-three per cent of the male cases. The total number of Canadians who have tested HIV positive is around 30,000.

2. "Can You Rely on Condoms?" *Consumer Reports*, 54, 3 (March, 1989), 135-141. A recent study found that of 405 condoms used for intercourse, 7 (1.7%) broke during intercourse or withdrawal, 25 (6.2%) slipped off during intercourse, and 27 (7.2%) slipped off during withdrawal. See James Trussell, David Lee Warner and Robert A. Hatcher, "Condom Slippage and Breakage Rates," *Family Planning Perspectives*, XXIV, 1 (January/February, 1992), 20-24.

3. Robert A. Hatcher, Felicia Stewart, Lames Trussell, Deborah Kowal, Felicia Guest, Gary K. Stewart, and Willard Cates, *Contraceptive Technology: 1990-1992*, 15th rev. ed., 133-135.

4. *Ibid.* Jones and Forrest, in their analysis of data from the 1988 National Survey of Family Growth (sample of 8,540 respondents), hold that the typical rates of failure for common methods of contraception are much higher, if they are corrected for the underreporting of abortion. Their corrected standardized typical failure rates were: combined pills 7.3%; condom 15.8%; diaphragm 22%; natural family planning methods 31.4%; and spermicides 30.2%. Higher typical failure rates were particularly found among teenagers and persons from families below 200% of the poverty level. See Elise F. Jones and Jacqueline Darroch Forrest, "Contraceptive Failure Rates Based on the 1988 NSFG," *Family Planning Perspectives*, XXIV, 1 (January/February, 1992), 12-19.

5. *Ibid.*

6. See June M. Reinisch, *The Kinsey Institute New Report on Sex*, 76-77.

Chapter Fourteen

1. Craig McKie, "Common-Law: Living Together as Husband and Wife without Marriage," *Canadian Social Trends* (Autumn 1986), 39-40.

2. Neil G. Bennett, Ann Klimas Blanc and David E. Bloom, "Commitment and the Modern Union: Assessing the Link between Premarital Cohabitation and Subsequent Marital Stability," *American Sociological Review*, 53 (February 1988), 127.

3. Koray Tanfer, "Patterns of Premarital Cohabitation among Never-Married Women in the United States," *Journal of Marriage and the Family*, 49 (August 1987), 485.

4. *Ibid.*, 132-133.

5. "We found that cohabiting prior to marriage, regardless of the nature of that cohabitation, is associated with an enhanced risk of later marital disruption. It appears that this association is beginning to take on the status of an *empirical generalization.*" (Italics mine) Alfred DeMaris and K. Vaninadha Rao, "Premarital Cohabitation and Subsequent Marital Stability in the United States: A Reassessment," *Journal of Marriage and the Family*, 54 (February 1992), 189. See Neil G. Bennett, Ann Klimas Blanc and David E. Bloom, "Commitment and the Modern Union: Assessing the Link between Premarital Cohabitation and Subsequent Marital Stability," *American Sociological Review*, 53 (February 1988), 127-138; Alan Booth and David Johnson, "Premarital Cohabitation and Marital Success," *Journal of Family Issues*, 9, 2 (June 1988), 255-271; Robert Schoen, "First Unions and Stability of First Marriages," *Journal of Marriage and the Family*, 54 (May 1992), 281-284. Jay D. Teachman and Karen A. Polonko, "Cohabitation and Marital Stability in the United States," *Social Forces*, 69, 1 (September 1990), 207-220; Elizabeth Thomson and Ugo Colella, "Cohabitation and Marital Stability: Quality or Commitment?" *Journal of Marriage and the Family*, 54 (May 1992), 259-267. A lone dissenting opinion can be found in James M. White, "Premarital Cohabitation and Marital Stability in Canada," *Journal of Marriage and the Family*, 49 (August 1987), 641-647. In response to criticism of his analysis by James Trussell and K. Vaninadha Rao, White revised his position in part, stating: "The reanalysis...shows that the effect for premarital cohabitation on marital stability for those whose first marriage is to their first cohabiting partner is now negative, as in the Trussell and Rao finding." James M. White, "Reply to Comment by Trussell and Rao: A Reanalysis of the Data," *Journal of Marriage and the Family*, 51 (May 1989), 540-544.

6. T.R. Balakrishnan, K.V. Rao, Evelyne Lapierre-Adamcyk, and Karol Krotki, "A Hazard Model Analysis of Marriage Dissolution in Canada'" *Demography*, (1987), 395-406.

7. Bennett, Blanc and Bloom, 132.

8. Teachman and Polonko, 211-212.

9. Alfred DeMaris and Gerald R. Leslie, "Cohabitation with the Future Spouse: Its Influence upon Marital Satisfaction and Communication," *Journal of Marriage and the Family*, 46 (February 1984), 77-84.

10. Booth and Johnson in the article cited above suggest that cohabitation itself may cause some of the adverse effects on marital success.

11. See Tanfer, 488.

12. Watson, 41. See Booth and Johnson, 270.

13. This position is supported by the data in Teachman and Polonko's article.

14. Bennett, Blanc and Bloom, 131-137. See DeMaris and Rao, 187-190.

15. Tanfer, 486.

16. *Ibid.*, 493.

17. Booth and Johnson, 256. Tanfer, 487-488.

18. See DeMaris and Leslie, 83; Bennett, Blanc and Bloom, 136; Booth and Johnson, 231; DeMaris and Rao, 189-190.

19. Schoen, 281-284.

20. Bennett, Blanc and Bloom, 132.

SELECTED BIBLIOGRAPHY

Achtemeier, Elizabeth R. *The Committed Marriage.* Philadelphia: Westminster Press, 1976.

Arond, Miriam, and Samuel L. Pauker. *The First Year of Marriage.* New York: Warner Books, 1987.

Bach, George S., and Peter Wyden. *The Intimate Enemy: How to Fight Fair in Love and Marriage.* New York: William Morrow & Co., 1969.

Balakrishnan, T.R., K.V. Rao, Evelyne Lapierre-Adamcyk, and Karol Krotki, "A Hazard Model Analysis of Marriage Dissolution in Canada," *Demography*, (1987), 395-406.

Bennett, Neil G., Ann Klimas Blanc and David E. Bloom, "Commitment and the Modern Union: Assessing the Link between Premarital Cohabitation and Subsequent Marital Stability," *American Sociological Review*, 53 (February 1988), 127-138.

Bernard, Jesse. *The Future of Marriage.* New York: Bantam Books, 1972.

Bertocci, Peter Anthony. *Sex, Love and the Person.* New York: Sheed and Ward, 1967.

Bird, Caroline. *The Two-Paycheck Marriage.* New York: Rawson Wade, 1979.

Bird, Joseph, and Lois Bird. *Marriage is for Grownups.* Garden City, New York: Doubleday, 1969.

Blumstein, Philip, and Pepper Schwartz. *American Couples: Money, Work, Sex.* New York: William Morrow, 1983.

Bly, Robert. *Iron John: A Book about Men.* Reading, Massachusetts: Addison-Wesley Publishing Company, Inc., 1990.

Booth, Alan, and David Johnson, "Premarital Cohabitation and Marital Success," *Journal of Family Issues*, 9, 2 (June 1988), 255-271.

Borysenko, Jean. *Guilt is the Teacher, Love is the Lesson.* New York: Warner Books, Inc., 1991

Bosco, Antoinette. *Marriage Encounter: The Rediscovery of Love.* St. Meinrad, Indiana: Abbey Press, 1972.

Botwin, Carol. *Is There Sex After Marriage?* New York: Pocket Books, 1985.

Brown, Helen Gurley. *Having It All: Love, Success, Sex, Money, Even If You're Starting With Nothing.* New York: Simon and Schuster, 1982.

Buijs, Joseph A., ed. *Christian Marriage Today: Growth or Breakdown? Interdisciplinary Essays.* New York: The Edward Mellen Press, 1985.

Bullough, Vern L., and Bonnie Bullough. *Contraception: A Guide to Birth Control Methods.* Buffalo, New York: Prometheus Books, 1990.

"Can you rely on Condoms?" *Consumer Reports*, March, 1989.

Carter, Steven, and Julia Sokol. *Men Who Can't Love.* New York: Berkley Books, 1988.

Clinebell, Charlotte H., and Howard J. Clinebell, Jr. *The Intimate Enemy.* New York: Harper & Row, 1970.

Cowan, Connell, and Melvyn Kinder. *Women Men Love, Women Men Leave: What Makes Men Want to Commit.* New York: Signet, 1987.

DeMaris, Alfred, and Gerald R. Leslie. "Cohabitation with the Future Spouse: Its Influence upon Marital Satisfaction and Communication," *Journal of Marriage and the Family*, 46 (February, 1984), 77-84.

DeMaris, Alfred, and K. Vaninadha Rao. "Premarital Cohabitation and Subsequent Marital Stability in the United States: A Reassessment," *Journal of Marriage and the Family*, 54 (February 1992), 178-190.

Dennis, Wendy. *Hot and Bothered: Men and Women, Sex and Love in the 90s.* Toronto: Key Porter Books Limited, 1992.

Dominian, Jack. *Marriage, Faith and Love.* London: Darton, Longman and Todd, 1981.

Ehrenreich, Barbara. *The Hearts of Men: American Dreams and the Flight from Commitment.* Garden City, N.Y.: Doubleday, 1983.

Farrell, Warren. *Why Men Are the Way They Are.* New York: McGraw-Hill, 1986.

Fels, Lynn. *Living Together: Unmarried Couples in Canada.* Toronto: Personal Library, 1981.

Ford, Edward E., with Robert L. Zorn. *Why Marriage?* Niles, Illinois: Argus Communications, 1974.

Frankl, Viktor E. *The Doctor and the Soul: From Psychotherapy to Logotherapy.* 2nd Ed. New York: Bantam Books, 1965.

Friedan, Betty. *The Feminine Mystique.* New York: W.W. Norton & Co., 1963.

_____. *The Second Stage*. New York: Summit Books, 1981.

Fromm, Erich. *The Art of Loving*. New York: Harper & Row 1956.

_____. *To Have or To Be*. New York: Harper & Row, 1976.

Gormely, Sheila. *Commitments: Intimate Stories of Love that Lasts*. Toronto: Doubleday, 1982.

Greeley, Andrew. *Love and Play*. Chicago: Thomas More Press, 1975.

_____. *Sexual Intimacy*. New York: Seabury Press, 1973.

Greenwald, Jerry G. *Creative Intimacy*. New York: Pyramid Books, 1975.

Greer, Germaine. *Sex & Destiny: The Politics of Human Fertility*. New York: Harper & Row, 1984.

Hart, Thomas N., and Kathleen Fischer Hart. *The First two Years of Marriage: Foundations for a Life Together*. New York: Paulist Press, 1983.

Hatcher, Robert A., Felicia Stewart, James Trussell, Deborah Kowal, Felicia Guest, Gary K. Stewart, and Willard Cates. *Contraceptive Technology: 1990-1992*. 15th rev. ed. New York: Irvington Publishers, 1990.

_____. *et al. Safely Sexual*. New York: Irvington Publishers, 1992.

Haughey, John C. *Should Anyone Say Forever: On Making, Keeping and Breaking Commitments*. Garden City, N.Y.: Image Books, 1977.

Hendrix, Harville. *Getting the Love You Want: A Guide for Couples*. New York: Henry Holt & Co., 1988.

Holmes, K.K., P-A Mardh, P.F. Sparling, P.J. Wiesner, W. Cates Jr., S.M. Lemon, and W.E. Stamm. *Sexually Transmitted Diseases*. 2nd ed. New York: McGraw-Hill Information Services Company, 1990.

Institute of Medicine, National Academy of Sciences. *Confronting AIDS: Directions for Public Health, Health Care, and Research*. Washington, D.C.: National Academy Press, 1986.

Johnson, Catherine. *Lucky in Love: The Secrets of Happy Couples and How Their Marriages Thrive*. New York: Viking, 1992.

Jones, Elise F. and Jacqueline Darroch Forrest. "Contraceptive Failure Rates Based on the 1988 NSFG," *Family Planning Perspectives*, XXIV, 1 (January/February 1992), 12-19.

Jourard, Sidney. *The Transparent Self: Self-Disclosure and Well Being*. Princeton: D. Van Nostrand Company, Inc., 1964.

Keen, Sam. *Fire in the Belly: On Being a Man.* New York: Bantam Books, 1992.

_____. *The Passionate Life: Stages of Loving.* New York: Harper & Row, 1983.

Klagsbrun, Francine. *Married People: Staying Together in the Age of Divorce.* New York: Bantam Books, 1985.

Landis, Paul H. *Making the Most of Marriage.* 5th ed. Englewood Cliffs, New Jersey: Prentice-Hall, Inc., 1975

Lederer, William J., and Don Jackson. *Mirages of Marriage.* New York: W.W. Norton & Co., 1968.

Lerner, Harriet Goldhor. *The Dance of Anger: A Woman's Guide to Changing the Pattern of Intimate Relationships.* New York: Harper & Row, 1985.

_____. *The Dance of Intimacy: A Woman's Guide to Courageous Acts of Change in Key Relationships.* New York: Harper & Row, 1989.

Lewis, C.S. *The Four Loves.* London: Fontana Books, 1963.

Mace, David. *Getting Ready for Marriage.* Nashville, Tennessee: Abingdon, 1972.

_____. *Love and Anger in Marriage.* Grand Rapids, Michigan: Zondervan Publishing House, 1982.

Mace, David, and Vera Mace. *How to Have a Happy Marriage.* Nashville, Tennessee: Abingdon, 1979.

_____. *We Can Have Better Marriages-If We Want Really Want Them.* Nashville, Tennessee: Abingdon, 1974.

Marcel, Gabriel. *Creative Fidelity.* trans. Robert Rosthal. New York: Crossroads, 1982.

Marty, Martin E. *Friendship.* Allen, Texas: Argus Communications, 1980.

Maslow, Abraham. *Toward a Psychology of Being.* Princeton: Van Nostrand, 1962.

Masters, William H., and Virginia E. Johnson. *The Pleasure Bond.* Boston: Little, Brown & Co., 1975.

May, Rollo. *Love and Will.* New York: Dell Publishing, Laurel Book, 1969.

McKie, Craig. "Common-Law: Living Together as Husband and Wife without Marriage," *Canadian Social Trends* (Autumn 1986), 39-41.

Naifeh, Steven, and Gregory White Smith. *Why Can't Men Open Up?* New York: Warner Books, 1984.

Norwood, Robin. *Women Who Love Too Much: When You Keep Wishing and Hoping He'll Change.* New York, Pocket Books, 1985.

O'Brien, Patricia. *Staying Together: Marriages That Work.* New York: Random House, 1977.

O'Neill, Nena, and George O'Neill. *Open Marriage*. New York: M. Evans and Company, Inc., 1972.

_____. *Shifting Gears: Finding Security in a Changing World.* New York: M. Evans and Company, Inc., 1974

Otto, Herbert A., ed. *Love Today: A New Exploration.* New York: Dell Publishing Co., Inc. A Delta Book, 1972.

Pietropinto, Anthony, and Jacqueline Seminauer. *Husbands and Wives: a Nation-wide Survey of Marriage.* New York: Times Books, 1979.

Pogrebin, Letty Cottin. *Family Politics: Love and Power on an Intimate Frontier.* New York: McGraw-Hill, 1983.

Posner, Judith. *The Feminine Mistake: Women, Work and Identity.* New York: Warner Books, Inc., 1992.

Powell, S.J., John. *Unconditional Love.* Niles, Illinois: Argus Communications, 1978.

Quackenbush, Marcia, and Mary Nelson with Kay Clark, eds. *The Aids Challenge: Prevention Education for Young People.* Santa Cruz, California: Network Publications, 1988.

Reinisch, June M. with Ruth Beasley. *The Kinsey Institute New Report on Sex: What You Must Know to be Sexually Literate.* New York: St. Martin's Press, 1990.

Rice, David G. *Dual-Career Marriage.* New York: Free Press, 1979.

Rubin, Lillian B. *Intimate Strangers: Men and Women Together.* New York: Harper & Row, 1983.

_____. *Just Friends: The Role of Friendship in Our Lives.* New York: Harper & Row, 1985.

Scarf, Maggie. *Intimate Partners: Patterns in Love and Marriage.* New York: Random House, 1987.

Schiappa, Barbara D. *Mixing: Catholic-Protestant Marriages in the 1980's.* New York: Paulist Press, 1982.

Schoen, Robert. "First Unions and the Stability of First Marriages," *Journal of Marriage and the Family*, 54 (May 1992), 281-284.

Simon, Sidney B., and Suzanne Simon. *Forgiveness: How to Make Peace with Your Past and Get on With Your Life.* New York: Warner Books,1990.

Skolnick, Arlene S. *The Intimate Environment: Exploring Marriage and the Family.* Boston: Little, Brown & Co., 1987.

Spanier, Graham. "Married and Unmarried Cohabitation in the United States: 1980," *Journal of Marriage and the Family*, 45 (May 1983), 277-288.

Tanfer, Koray. "Patterns of Premarital Cohabitation among Never-Married Women in the United States," *Journal of Marriage and the Family*, 49 (August 1987), 483-497.

Teachman, Jay D., and Karen A. Polonko, "Cohabitation and Marital Stability in the United States," *Social Forces*, 69, 1 (September 1990), 207-220.

Tennov, Dorothy. Love and Limerence. *The Experience of Being in Love.* New York: Stein and Day. Scarborough Book, 1979.

Thomson, Elizabeth, and Ugo Colella. "Cohabitation and Marital Stability: Quality or Commitment?" *Journal of Marriage and the Family*, 54 (May, 1992), 259-267.

Trussell, James, and K. Vaninadha Rao, "Premarital Cohabitation and Marital Stability: A Reassessment of the Canadian Evidence," *Journal of Marriage and the Family*, 51 (May 1989), 535-539.

Trussell, James, David Lee Warner and Robert A. Hatcher. "Condom Slippage and Breakage Rates," *Family Planning Perspectives*, XXIV, 1 (January/February 1992), 20-23.

Vaughan, Diane. *Uncoupling: Turning Points in Intimate Relationships.* New York: Oxford University Press, 1986.

Viscott, David. *The Language of Feelings: The Time-and-Money Shorthand of Psychotherapy.* New York: Arbor House, 1976.

_____. *How to Live with Another Person.* New York: Arbor House, 1974.

_____. *I Love You: Let's Work It Out.* New York: Pocket Books, 1987.

Watson, Roy E.L. "Premarital Cohabitation vs. Traditional Courtship: Their Effects on Subsequent Marital Adjustment," *Family Relations*, 32 (January 1983), 139-146.

Westheimer, Ruth, and Louis Lieberman. *Sex and Morality: Who is Teaching Our Sex Standards?* New York: Harcourt Brace Jovanovich, Publishers, 1988.

White, James M. "Premarital Cohabitation and Marital Stability in Canada," *Journal of Marriage and the Family*, 49 (August 1987), 641-647.

_____. "Reply to Comment by Trussell and Rao: A Reanalysis of the Data," *Journal of Marriage and the Family*, 51 (May 1989), 540-544.

INDEX